THE FOUR QUADRANTS
TO GREATNESS.

Walking In Kingdom Dominion.

OWUSU AMOATENG KOFI

xulon
PRESS

Copyright © 2015 by OWUSU AMOATENG KOFI

THE FOUR QUADRANTS TO GREATNESS.
Walking In Kingdom Dominion.
by OWUSU AMOATENG KOFI

Printed in the United States of America.

ISBN 9781498436861

All rights reserved solely by the author. The author guarantees all contents are original and do not infringe upon the legal rights of any other person or work. No part of this book may be reproduced in any form without the permission of the author. The views expressed in this book are not necessarily those of the publisher.

Unless otherwise indicated, Scripture quotations taken from the Holy Bible, New Living Translation. Copyright ©1996, 2004, 2007 by Tyndale House Foundation. Used by permission of Tyndale House Publishers, Inc.

www.xulonpress.com

CONTENTS

Dedication vii
Introduction ix

AN OVERVIEW

Chapter 1   The Process of W.A.L.K.I.N.G 17
Keys to Walking
The Four Kingdoms

Chapter 2   The Dominion Mandate 32
The seed principle
Be results oriented
Never be full of leafs
Areas of fruitfulness
Principles and promises
How to multiply fruits
Powers that seek to conquer you

QUADRANT 1 – BE FRUITFUL

Chapter 3   The Power of Knowing Yourself 62
Dangers of lack of self-awareness

Chapter 4   The Power of Imagination 88
Components of your imagination
Components of your thought
What the mind need to fulfill quadrant one
Thinking skills of quadrant one people

QUADRANT 2 – MULTIPLY

Chapter 5   The Power of Choice 112
How to make the right choices in life
Choosing your chosen destiny
Choosing to multiply your fruits

Chapter 6   The Power of Change 132
God changes things
How to make relevant changes
What makes people not to change

QUADRANT 3 – REPLENISH

Chapter 7   The Power of Focus 152
Focus defined
Focus on purpose
The 80/20 principle
What to focus on

QUADRANT 4 – SUBDUE

Chapter 8   The Power of Faith 170
Proving your faith

Chapter 9   The Power of the Holy Spirit 190
The purpose of the anointing
Key to the anointing
Vitality of the anointing

RENEWAL

Chapter 10   The Power of Love 212
Men who build lasting legacy
What is love?
Living and walking in love

Acknowledgement 233

DEDICATION

I dedicate this book especially to my dear and virtuous wife Rhoda Owusu and our three (3) wonderful children, Christine, Ephraim and Immanuel for your love and support. You all are Gods greatest gift to me.

I also dedicate this book to the memories of the late **Dr. Myles Munroe** for being an inspiration to my discovery of assignment in life and fulfilling it.

INTRODUCTION

Dear beloved, welcome to this great manifesto for effective living. A book is simply an idea container. This simply means that you are holding in your hands a tool which has the capacity to give you what you need or quicken you to transform your life into a whole new dimension.

The purpose of this book is to get you to walk in your Kingdom dominion mandate by realizing your already endowed ability from the Creator which is the four quadrant system you are about to discover. In other to realize this, it is first of all important to understand the process of walking. Why? Because dominion or power is not something we just talk about, neither is it something that will easily come to us. Even though God has created you with endowed capacities and abilities, it takes a process, technique and effort to fulfill potential.

In this introduction, I take time to explain to you what this book really means and what should be your expectation as you pick it up to read. Therefore, to get the best from this book, you must understand its roots and fruits through the following:

1. Slumber (Ignorance)

The first group of people this book is calling on is those -in slumber. You can never walk in dominion if you are in slumber. The word 'slumber' can simply be defined as *a state of being asleep*. To thrust deeper, it is also to be in a state of *negligence, sloth, supineness, and inactivity*. As Editor James Terry White carefully said, *"nature has everywhere written her protest against idleness; everything which ceases to struggle towards an ideal remains inactive, rapidly deteriorates. It is the struggle toward an ideal, the constant effort to get higher and further, which develops manhood and character."*

The definitions above lead us to four key characteristics of a person in slumber we cannot overlook.

a) Negligence speaks of failure to take proper care in doing something that can result in damage or loss of asset. For instance, failing to use endowed abilities in you may result not only in disappointing yourself but an entire generation. The purpose of this book therefore is to get you out of negligence and challenge you to fulfilling potential in your life, business, ministry, and family.

b) *Slothfulness* simply means laziness. It is also defined as physical, spiritual or emotional apathy, overlooking what God has spoken, and being physically and emotionally inactive. This is dangerous and people who do not change:

I. **End up in poverty and scarcity**: *"So how long are you going to laze around doing nothing? How long before you get out of bed? A nap here, a nap there, a day off here, a day off there, sit back, take it easy—do you know what comes next? Just this: You can look forward to a dirt-poor life, poverty your permanent houseguest."* **Proverbs 6:9-10 (MSG)**

Introduction

II. **End up not tapping into what God has given them**. In the parable of the talents, this is what happened to the one with one gift. Read **Matthew 25:14-30** and get understanding. It states (v 24-26, NLT) *"²⁵ I was afraid I would lose your money, so I hid it in the earth. Look, here is your money back.'²⁶ "But the master replied, 'You wicked and lazy servant! If you knew I harvested crops I didn't plant and gathered crops I didn't cultivate, ²⁷ why didn't you deposit my money in the bank? At least I could have gotten some interest on it.'*

III. **End up not taking what God has endowed them to the next level**: this category is the most serious of them all. *"The slothful man roasteth not that which he took in hunting: but the substance of a diligent man is precious."* **Proverbs 12:27 (KJV)**. A perfect example is Esau, the brother of Jacob, who one day came back home from hunting exusted but failed to curb his appetite without considering the long range effect of his actions due to laziness.. He ended up selling his dominion mandate for a plate of food from his brother.

c) Supineness: This refers to person(s) with sloping-backward mentality and attitude. These people are in slumber because they fail to maximize time when most necessary. It is failing to act based on God's abilities given to us because of moral weakness or indolence.

d) Inactivy: These are people who are not active; not engaging in or involving much physical activity. They are those who are not working even though they can work. Work is in a sense what you do for the benefit of others and not yourself. So if there is something you can do to benefit mankind but you are not doing, you are inactive.

This is why **Ambrose Bierce** said *"a total abstainer is one who abstains from everything but abstention, and especially from inactivity in the affairs of others."* Inactive people cannot walk in their dominion mandate. Inactivity is as good as being dead. God never created man to retire, we cannot stop working. We cannot stop solving problems; in fact man is a problem-solving machine. This is why a man is active until he retires. Retirement can lead to inactivity, which can lead to one's demise.

Part of the root causes of stress, depression, worry, anxiety and more is physical inactivity. These diseases today are the cause of death in many people because there is no perfect medication for them. The real remedy is to activate your God-given dominion; anything else will not hold without this.

A lot of people cannot walk into their dominion mandate because they are in this state of slumber. It is like having gold and not realising the value and power in it. Ignorance is not an excuse. For lack of knowledge, my people perish, the Bible says. *Not knowing who you are in life is like having eyes that cannot see and ears that cannot hear.*

To people in this category, the only solution is to *awake*.

2. Awake. (Information)

To awake is *simply to wake up from your sleep or a slumber*. In other words, if you do not know who you are and what you have, this book has been written to inform and help you discover your God-endowed ability by waking you up from slumber. Indeed, the best way to make a sluggish mind active is through challenging oneself to begin to think outside the box.

To awake therefore is a self-initiative action. This means no one can wake you up unless you are ready. **Henry David Thoreau** *once* *said "We must learn to reawaken and keep ourselves awake, not by mechanical aid, but by an infinite expectation of the dawn."* The question therefore is, are you ready to wake up?

Though this book is written for everybody, I cannot help but call on the body of Christ especially to wake up to the call of God and pray and preach. We cannot continue to sleep and expect the work to be done.

"When he came back to his disciples, he found them sound asleep. He said to Peter, "Can't you stick it out with me a single hour? Stay alert; be in prayer so you don't wander into temptation without even knowing you're in danger. There is a part of you that is eager, ready for anything in God. But there's another part that's as lazy as an old dog sleeping by the fire." **Matthew 26:40-41** (MSG)

The danger for people in this category is this: you can wake up and not arise.

3. Arise (understanding)

To those who are awakening, prepare yourself to walk. To do this you must first get ready to arise. People in this category are not in slumber (ignorance), they have awoken (information). To arise therefore is to use your endowed abilities to change things because nothing changes until we change.

No wonder this is the best position to be in if you are to walk in the four (4) quadrant system or principle for your life, business, church and more. *To arise is to get up from sitting down. It demonstrates readiness and preparedness to move.* The first step to shining in your field of work is by arising. Rising up also demonstrates a state of being ready to act.

The Four Quadrants To Greatness.

"Get out of bed, Jerusalem! Wake up. Put your face in the sunlight. God's bright glory has risen for you" **Isaiah 60:1(MSG)**. **Ephesians 5:14** sums it all up when Paul said, *"For the light makes everything visible. This is why it is said, "Awake, O sleeper, rise up from the dead, and Christ will give you light."*

Arising is also a self-initiative action. However, you can arise and not walk.

4. Walking

This book seeks to get you to walk in your endowed dominion. You are endowed to be *fruitful, multiply, replenish* and *subdue*. I call these the four quadrants to greatness and God has ordained every human being to succeed. Every great man you can pin point today has gone through these four significant processes mandated by God.

Together, I have built a system called, *The Four Quadrant Kingdom Dominion System*™, which is to be unveiled in the chapters of this book. Below is a complete picture of the system.

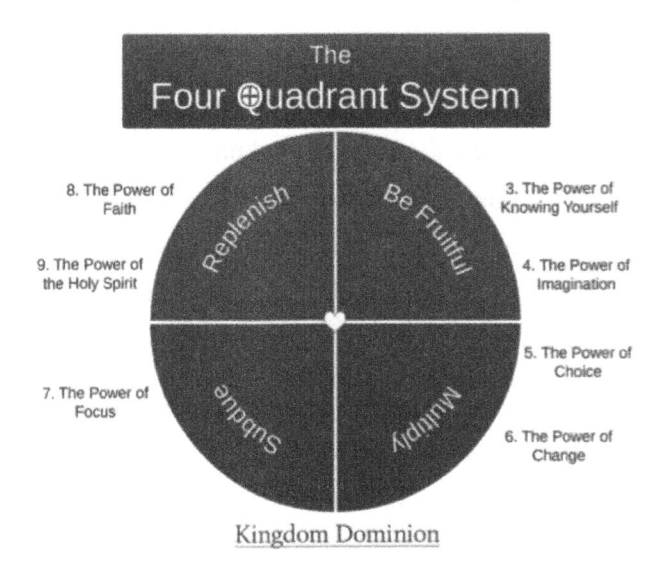

The Four Quadrant System

- 8. The Power of Faith
- 9. The Power of the Holy Spirit
- 3. The Power of Knowing Yourself
- 4. The Power of Imagination
- 5. The Power of Choice
- 6. The Power of Change
- 7. The Power of Focus

Quadrants: Replenish, Be Fruitful, Multiply, Subdue

Kingdom Dominion

The first two chapters in the book further gives you more information about The Four Quadrant Kingdom Dominion System™ as it prepares you to harness the principles into your life and organisation.

My **prayer** for you as you breathe through the root and fruit of this book is that **God will permit you to taste real dominion in your life time. Amen.**

I
THE PROCESS OF WALKING

There are two animals God uses to describe some aspects of Himself. These are the lion and the eagle. The lion is fiercely known as the king of the jungle, whereas the eagle is the king of the air. Both of these animals demonstrate to us what it means to walk and even fly in dominion. The lion's courage, confidence, persistence, self-esteem and positive thinking are what qualify it to rule as the king of the jungle. The strength and especially the vision of the eagle are comparable to none.

If God associates with these creatures because of some of these qualities, then the man or woman who desires to walk in dominion must learn from these animals. We are actually created to walk in dominion and this is what this book seeks to achieve; to convince, challenge and empower you to discover your dominion mandate and be all you can be.

> The lion's courage, confidence, persistent, self-esteem and positive thinking are what qualify it to rule as the king of the jungle.

The dictionary defines *walking* as *a process of moving over a surface by taking steps with the feet at a pace slower than a run or the action of one that moves. It is also regarded as having the capabilities or qualities of a specified object.*

Judging from these definitions, we can instigate that walking is both a process and a technique. As a process, it involves movements and taking actions where you add something or subtract from it or making exchanges and trade-offs in other to gain results.

Secondly, the process of walking also includes you developing your in-built capabilities and qualities. Just as one cannot walk without the physical mechanism and ability to walk, so it is in any major success you desire to achieve. You have been born with good qualities to succeed, but it remains your responsibility to embrace and develop your creativity.

Thirdly, there must be a surface to move over or an object to pursue. This is where technique comes into action. There is no reward in aimless pursuit. You must have a primary purpose for who you are and what you do. In other words, you must have a vision of what you want and develop a curiosity mindset to find ways of getting there. Our object to pursue most of the time is outside our self-imposed boxes and requires us getting out of ourselves in order to get things done.

Keys to walking

Permit me to use the acronym of W.A.L.K.I.N.G to prepare you to transform your life by getting you ready to take dominion. The process of walking begins when you center your life on correct principles. Why? Because correct principles do not change and we can depend on them. Below are such principles.

W- Worship:

The first key to walking in your dominion mandate is to seek to worship. To worship could also simply means to serve and service is the rent we pay for what we want to enjoy on earth. Whatever you are using here on earth, you pay for its services one way or another. For instance, to enjoy the benefit of a degree, I must pay my way through university, to build a house, I must pay for the land or pay monthly rent or mortgage, to benefit effectively from my phone, I must pay for my services either on contract or pay-as-you-go.

This is why worship is the number one requirement in everything we do. One of God's key requirements from everything He has created is worship. God does not need anything from us other than sincere worship from our hearts. This explains why to religious people, our meetings are called worship services. Worship service is to God as customer service is to customers. Every thriving and successful business or organization must learn to serve its customers right and with excellence. Have you heard of the saying that the customer is always right? This is just to emphasise the power of worship.

> God does not need anything from us other than sincere worship from our hearts

For you to provide uncompromising worship to God or serve customers, one must also understand the need to be patient. We must endeavour to develop good character and a personal or team culture to wait on God or the people in our organisations and businesses. You will walk in your endowed kingdom dominion and authority when you first learn to worship God with all your heart, mind and soul and secondly when you serve the world with your gift, talent, and capacity, leadership in business, academics, family, society and nation.

A- Agree:

The second key to walking in dominion is to prepare to agree with the principles and laws laid since God created the world. Principles are natural laws that are external to us and ultimately control our actions. They operate regardless of our ignorance, awareness, belief, like or dislike of them.

This book is based on godly principles which, when agreed to, have the capacity of transforming your life, family, career, ministry and business. The principles taught in this book are based on God's first commandment to man to be *fruitful, multiply, replenish and subdue*.

Can two people walk together without agreeing on the direction? Walking in agreement with these timeless principles and laws will lead you to goodwill and team work in your businesses and ministries. It will also lead to companionship and fellowship in marriage relationships. Above all, countries and nations will enjoy commonwealth prosperity.

L- Live in God's love

The third key to walking in dominion is to learn to walk and live in God's love towards you. The love of God towards you, not your love towards Him, is your strongest and most effective weapon spiritually and even physically. I wonder if you agree with me on this. Nothing can destroy the man or woman who feeds on this truth.

> Love is the fabric that holds everything together

One major anchor you will be discovering in this book is how not to only know but also understand and begin to live in God's love concerning your marriage, career, ministry and everything you represent and beyond.

The Process of Walking

There is a whole chapter teaching you about the extent and unlimited nature of God's wonderful love towards you and how living and walking in love will help you to subdue every obstacle on your way to success. Truthfully, love is the fabric that holds everything together and without love I doubt whether man can succeed in any endeavour. Seek to do what you love and love what you do.

K- Knowing Christ

The fourth key to walking in your dominion mandate lies in knowing Christ and knowing Him more. Paul once said, that *"I may know Him and the power of His resurrection."* **Philippians 3:10**. There is a reason why this intellectual with all his degrees and accomplishment sought to know Christ.

This book is about the power and authority that has been bestowed on you and how best to understand this by connecting yourself to the source of this power. Knowing Christ is the foundation and basis for knowing His power.

Christ is the visible image of the invisible God. He existed before anything was created and is supreme over all creation,[a]16 for through him God created everything in the heavenly realms and on earth. He made the things we can see and the things we can't see— such as thrones, kingdoms, rulers, and authorities in the unseen world. Everything was created through him and for him.17 He existed before anything else, and he holds all creation together. **Colossians 1:15-17 (NLT)**

I- Increase:

The fifth key to walk in kingdom dominion is to seek to increase. To increase is simply to ascend through processes of growth. It retards stagnancy and laziness. The principles you are about to discover have the capacity of increasing and propelling you into greater heights.

The process of increasing therefore involves moving from one stage to another. When you take these principles for instance, you will learn that, there cannot be fruitfulness without sowing a seed, neither can there be multiplication without fruits or replenishment without multiplication and certainly can one not subdue without replenishing. Therefore to understand the principle of increase strongly involves you to comprehend interdependence and connection between these principles.

N- Now

The sixth key to walking in kingdom dominion is to understand the now moment. This moment is that of sudden, immediate and ultimate breakthrough. Your time of manifestation has come because nothing works like obeying laws and principles. As you begin to practice these principles, I can confidently comfort you that your time of manifestation has come with no more delay. These principles are designed to set things right in your life, not in the distant future but right now.

G- Great Grace, Great Power

The seventh key to walking in kingdom dominion is through great Grace. It takes Grace to fulfill the principles and laws that have originally been set even before the foundation of this world. Grace is unmerited favor. It is something that makes one different from another. The grace of God is not the opportunity to be lazy and yet expect results, it goes beyond that.

Grace actually is an empowerment to begin to do things your natural strength cannot do. You have been wired for greatness and it is my prayer that God will grant you the ability to walk in your endowed dominion mandate. In fact, there is sufficient grace for the rest of your life. God knows that you will need help as you progress in life and so has made His help ready through His Chief Executive Officer (Holy Spirit) to empower you whenever the need arises in your walk in dominion. Such is the power of great grace.

> Grace is an empowerment to begin to do things your natural strength cannot do.

❖

The word dominion is mostly familiar in Kingdom settings and one way or the other; we are all citizens of kingdoms, countries and nations. This book introduces you to kingdom authority as you begin to breathe through its pages and since we are all product of a kingdom, it is important that you comprehend its meaning, even in the 21st Century world. Every kingdom is defined and comprises a king, a people and a territory which defines the jurisdiction of the king. We all have been created and in one way or the other are influenced by kingdom principles. There are four main types of Kingdoms you should permit me through this book to introduce you to since fulfilling the quadrants equals to Kingdom dominion.

1. Kingdom of God:

This is the first and most important kingdom of all. It is where God, the Creator of everything, dwells. As a matter of truth, all principles shared in this book come from God's Kingdom. It exists in eternity and functions by speaking the Word of God and bringing from it. It is a mystery that has not been fully revealed to the physical eyes. The purpose of Jesus Christ coming was to reconnect mankind to this powerful Kingdom.

> The strength or weakness of every kingdom lies in the standard of living of its citizens.

Therefore he taught, preached, demonstrated and manifested God's Kingdom on earth. One of His immediate public statements states thus: *"Therefore take no thought, saying, What shall we eat? or, What shall we drink? or, Wherewithal shall we be clothed? But seek ye first the kingdom of God, and his righteousness; and all these things shall be added unto you.* **Matthew 6:31,33. (KJV)**

Maslow's hierarchy of need is a theory in Psychology proposed by Abraham Maslow. According to Maslow, the most fundamental (first and most important) needs of every human being are physiological needs such as food, water, and clothing. To Maslow, for every man to achieve self- actualization (full potential, creativity), man must first be satisfied physiologically.

While Maslow is right to a degree, Jesus' statement above teaches us something deeper. To Jesus, seeking physiological needs as proposed by Maslow must not be the fundamental goal of every man. Rather, every human being must seek first the Kingdom of God and then all other things (food, water and cloth) and even more shall be added to them. Is there any validity or truth in what Jesus is saying?

The strength or weakness of every kingdom lies in the standard of living of its citizens. In other words, you can determine the level of influence a kingdom, country, business or a family has by looking at its citizens or members. Jesus reveals therefore to us that the Kingdom of God is fundamental or key to us because its citizens shall never lack food, cloth, water, a good future or any other thing.

This is why one day, a renowned citizen of God's Kingdom, a man called David, said, *"Once I was young, and now I am old. Yet I have never seen the godly abandoned or their children begging for bread."* **Psalm 37:25 (NLT).** David confirms the statement of Jesus by proving to us that, it is never possible for citizens of God's kingdom to be begging or lacking any good thing. Are you a citizen of this Kingdom? I challenge a reader of this book to use any internet search engine and discover for yourself more about Jesus and God's kingdom.

2. The Kingdom of Satan

Oh yes, Satan also has a kingdom and whether you believe it or not it is still standing. It is a high-powered kingdom with far-above-the-ground intelligence. It is the only kingdom that is united not by love but hatred. There is no love in the camp of the enemy yet for them to achieve their purpose of stealing, killing and destroying man, they are united **(John 10:10).** They do not tolerate division but their mandate is division.

In **Matthew 12:25-28 (NLT)**, Jesus makes mention and reveals clearly the kingdom of Satan in this way. Jesus knew their thoughts and replied, *"Any kingdom divided by civil war is doomed. A town or family splintered by feuding will fall apart. ²⁶ And if Satan is casting out Satan, he is divided and fighting against himself. <u>His own kingdom</u> will not survive. ²⁷ And if I am empowered by Satan, what about your own exorcists? They cast out demons, too, so they* will condemn you for what you have said. ²⁸ But if I am casting out demons by the Spirit of God, then <u>the Kingdom of God</u> has arrived among you."

For his kingdom to survive therefore, Satan functions through deception, discouragement, doubt and denial, in order to steal, kill and destroy your family, marriage, ministry, career and business. The only way to overcome this demonic kingdom is by becoming a citizen in God's kingdom, which helps you to raise the standard against him.

3. Kingdom of the world

"Then the devil took him up and revealed to him all the kingdoms of the world in a moment of time. ⁶ "I will give you the glory of these kingdoms and authority over them," the devil said, "because they are mine to give to anyone I please." **Luke 4:5-6 (NLT)**

This is an encounter between Jesus and Satan and in this meeting we discover the kingdoms of the world. This world is mine not God's, Satan was saying, and the fact that Jesus did not argue with Satan here about who owns the world is a proof that at this moment in time Satan is the king of this world. *"We know that we are children of God and that <u>the world around us is under the control of the evil one.</u>"* **1 John 5:19 (KJV)**

Indeed, if you observe the trends in the world today, especially in the areas of music, fashion and technology, it is without doubt that Satan influences the ideals, opinions, goals, hopes and views of those who are in his domain. His influence also permeates the world's philosophies, education, thoughts, ideas, speculations and false religions of the world, which he pioneers through lies, deceptions, discouragements, doubts and distraction.

However, it is important to note that the authority of Satan as the god of this world is limited to unbelievers. "Satan, who is the god of this world, has blinded the minds of those who don't believe. They are unable to see the glorious light of the Good News. They don't understand this message about the glory of Christ, who is the exact likeness of God." 2 Corinthians 4:4 (NLT).

His control over the world does not stretch to those under God's dominion. God's Kingdom is still sovereign and believers are not under Satan's dominion but God's. *"For he has rescued us from the **kingdom of darkness** and transferred us into the **Kingdom of his dear Son**, [14] who purchased our freedom[a] and forgave our sins."* Colossians 1:13-14 (NLT).

The question as you read this book is, under whose dominion do you desire to walk? This book promotes God's dominion mandate among mankind over Satan's kingdom. For further readings on the kingdom of Satan, read Ephesians 2:2, John 12:31, 2 Timothy 2:26, 1 John 2:15-16.

4. Kingdom of men

This is the kingdom where God's authority and power is reflected in an individual He wills to give dominion to. It is the demonstration of God's Kingdom dominion in righteousness, peace, joy in the Holy Ghost and not just in words, so as to bring forth fruitfulness, multiplication, replenishment and subduing, as evidence of His power and authority from within an individual.

This is good news for those seeking first the Kingdom of God and its righteousness; God rules in all their affairs by permitting them to evidently taste and walk in His Kingdom Dominion. There are many examples from scriptures but permit me to use three (3) major ones to demonstrate to you what this means.

The first is about a young man called **Daniel,** who was distinguished among many. God chose him to demonstrate His dominion in his generation because he was a Kingdom citizen.

" This decision is by the decree of the watchers, And the sentence by the word of the holy ones, In order that the living may know That the Most High rules in the kingdom of men, Gives it to whomever He will, And sets over it the lowest of men" **Daniel 4:17 (NKJV)**

You may be the lowest, weakest, insignificant (name it) man in your family, school, business, society or country, yet God can turn things completely around for your good.

The second example is Moses, a stammerer, a man of low self-esteem, who did not see anything good in himself, yet when the Most High began to rule in him, he became like a god unto obstacles and challenges of destiny. Then the LORD said to Moses, *"Pay close attention to this. I will make you seem like God to Pharaoh, and your brother, Aaron, will be your prophet.* **Exodus 7:1 (NLT)**

Another man God ruled in his affairs and granted kingdom dominion is David. The least among his brethren, he was selected from being just common to be a king. God anointed and empowered him to be strong by His hand.

> Without God's help, we are weak and powerless even in the simplest of tasks.

He (David) displayed and demonstrated kingdom dominion among nations. In the kingdom of men, God's grace can make a difference in your life, family, business and everything you represent.

Without God's help, we are weak and powerless even in the simplest of tasks, but when God-given dominion is reflected in you, just like David you shall display power by becoming a leader among the nations. You shall command nations to obey and they will come running before you. Why? Because the King of all kings rules in the affairs of men and has made you glorious. For more about David, read 1 Samuel 16, 17, Isaiah 55: 1-8, 2 Samuel 8:1-16, Psalm 89: 19

When God rules in the kingdom of men:
- ❖ Everyone has a gift
- ❖ Everyone is born for a primary purpose
- ❖ Everyone has a level of grace
- ❖ Everyone has an anointing to fulfill all assignments.
- ❖ Everyone has time to fulfill his or her assignment

This is the purpose of this book. To pick up your gift and purpose and by the special strength of God to be not only fruitful in your assignment but also in time multiply, replenish and subdue the world and satanic kingdoms under your feet.

I prophecy unto your life and destiny that you are next in line for what God can do in the kingdom of men. May you reflect God's glory here on earth by managing the resources He has bestowed on you. As you read this book, may your faith, life, family, career, business, ministry all change to taste God's dominion mandate.

APPLYING THE PROCESS OF WALKING TO YOUR LIFE

1. The process of WALKING begins with developing your in-built capabilities and qualities. Discover and embrace your creativity.
2. Understand that walking in dominion is a process, not a technique. To begin the process, identify your primary purpose and take responsibility for your gifts. Develop a lion and eagle attitude or mindset.
3. Discover, develop and embrace your understanding of what it means to manifest the mnemonics of **W.A.L.K.I.N.G**
   - **Worship**: Learn to serve
   - **Agreement**: Walk in correct principles
   - **Live in God's love**: This is your strongest and effective weapon
   - **Know Christ**: Connect your family, business, life and destiny to the source of life.
   - **Increase**: Move from stagnancy and laziness and increase your life and destiny.
   - **Grace**: Receive the power and super ability to do what you have been wired to do.
4. Reread the pages of the four (4) kingdoms and consider the following:
   - **Kingdom of God**: The strength of every kingdom lies in the standard of living of its citizens. Are you a citizen of God's kingdom?
   - **Kingdom of Satan**: The kingdom united not by love but hatred. Consider the state of your heart and where you are now

- ❖ **Kingdom of the World**: In what ways do worldly music, fashion, technology, etc. play a part in your life?
- ❖ **Kingdom of men**: Do the authority and dominion of God rule in your affairs? In what ways can you include or improve God's authority in your family, business, career and more?

5. Finally, in the kingdom of men, everyone has something God can use to do greater and marvelous things.
    - ❖ Identify your gifts both physical and spiritual
    - ❖ Discover why you are born for such a time like this (purpose)
    - ❖ Pray for more grace
    - ❖ In what ways can you maximize your days on earth?

2

THE DOMINION MANDATE

The source of walking in Kingdom dominion is what this chapter is focusing on. You are about to discover the most important things in your life. God's original intention for creating man was to have dominion. When somebody tells you to have **dominion**, he is simply giving you permission to succeed. Every man on the surface of this earth has originally been mandated *to rule, take charge and be in control*.

After God had created man both male and female in His image, He spoke into man the power to rule and exercise control over the earth and indeed everything He has created. This is the source of man's dominion over the earth. Therefore in this chapter, we explore the first command of God to man and what it should mean to you.

> God's dominion mandate allows you to have access to everything but never to own them.

The law of first mention teaches that the first time a word is used should be taken with all seriousness; how much the first of the Almighty God to mankind. To really understand the endowed abilities you possess, you must seek and understand its origin. Without this, whatever the intent of this book is will be a facade to you.

The book of Genesis contains most first statements of God because it contains records of what happened in creation. Genesis simply means *beginnings or origin* and it unfolds records of the beginning of the world, human history, sin, government and salvation. It is therefore a book you must read with care in order to understand the foundation of everything and most importantly the power and purpose of God.

Some people do hold arguments and doubt about the creative genius of God, but the truth still needs to be told. The bible is about a Kingdom and in this Kingdom; God is the King as established in Chapter One. Those who believe are His people and in a Kingdom we obey the King's rules, commands and laws with no arguments because a King owns everything.

Now after God had created man, He did something significant and this is the bedrock of this book: your **dominion mandate.**

And God blessed them, and God said unto them, Be fruitful, and multiply, and replenish the earth, and subdue it: and have dominion over the fish of the sea, and over the fowl of the air, and over every living thing that moveth upon the earth.
Genesis 1:26-28

After God had patterned man after His likeness, He blessed us. To be *blessed* simply means *to have power to win*. This simply means that every area of curse in your life is not from God. In this verse, you discover the first commandment or instruction from God to man.

This mandate is for man to be **fruitful, multiply, replenish and subdue the earth**. In these four statements lie mankind's greatest abilities. This ability covers the fish of the sea, fowl of the air and every living thing that moves upon the surface of the earth. Man has total control over such, excluding your fellow man.

By God doing this, He set heaven for Himself and delegated earth to man. It is now our responsibility to handle this authority with care. There is no room for carelessness and excuses, as the owner is going to judge you for what you use this ability to do.

So it continued in the book of **Genesis 2:15** that God placed man in the Garden of Eden to tend and take care of it but never to own it. The reason has been that in the Kingdom of God, we can only have access to things but never own them. God's dominion mandate allows you to have access to everything but never to own them.

> The greatest seed one can sow is the seed of honour.

This is why everything in your possession is never yours to keep. Even your wife and children, clothes and all are in your keep temporarily. In the eyes of God, we are stewards of everything. My time, energy, money, cars all belong to God. The earth is the LORD'S and the fullness thereof. The word LORD simply means *owner*. There may be many landlords in the world, but there is only one Lord of Lords and that is Jehovah, the Owner of all owners.

This is why the spirit of ownership at the end has always resulted in limitation, depression, poverty and death. It is only the world system that encourages ownership, but in the Kingdom of God, only He is the Lord of lords. If you doubt this principle, observe the burial service of a dead man and ask yourself whether he is buried with his riches.

After Adam and Eve sinned, God banished them from the Garden of Eden. They no longer deserved the paradise God had created for mankind, yet the original mandate to *control, rule and have authority* was not taken from man. The mandate was reaffirmed to Noah after the flood **(Genesis 9:1–10),** with the additional institution of human government, a change made necessary by the entrance of sin and death into the world. Thus, all the occupations we now call the social sciences (law, civics, counselling, etc.) have been added to God's authorized vocations.

The Psalmist further confirms God's dominion over man when he recorded, *"⁴ What is man, that thou art <u>mindful of him</u>? and the son of man, that thou <u>visitest him</u>?⁵ For thou hast made him a little lower than the angels, and hast crowned him with <u>glory and honour</u>.⁶ Thou madest him to have <u>dominion</u> over the works of thy hands; thou hast put all things under his feet"* Psalm 8:4-6 (KJV)

What a powerful scripture if only you will understand its meaning. There are 4 things and permit me to enlarge

1. **God is mindful of man.**

    This means that God thinks of you. For God to think of you therefore means there is no doubt that He loves you if you are reading this book. There is no limit as to how God loves you and wants you to succeed. *"For I know the thought I think of you, a thought of good and not of evil, to bring you to an expected end."*

2. **God visits you.**

    This simply means God yearns to have a relationship with you. God created man for relationship right from the beginning. Even when this relationship was broken along the way, He revealed Himself through Jesus to restore that relationship.

3. **Every man is crowned with glory and honour.**

   The greatest seed one can sow is the seed of honour. You must honour God's gift and talent in you. You dishonour God when you fail to walk in your dominion mandate. Whenever you dishonour God, you disinherit His blessing which is the anointing (ability to perform supernaturally), spirit of revelation and visitation of God and rather invite curses in your life. This is part of the bedrock of this book, to warn generations from dishonouring God because the spirit of dishonour is robbing many of their inheritance and blessing.

4. **God has put you in charge of everything He has created.**
   You are a leader from the first day of your birth. Research has discovered that during sexual intercourse, millions of sperms are released into a woman and all these sperms fight for one egg.

   Today you are that sperm that was able to outrun all the others to your mother's egg. Now tell me whether you are not special and unique and all that God is saying about you is not true.

In this book, you will discover a deeper insight into each of the four mandates God has given all of mankind. All four mandates must be accomplished if you are to exercise complete dominion in every aspect of life. In other words, man's mandate to dominate is not complete until these four are realised.

From this point forward, we shall refer to these endowments as the four (4) quadrants, because these four (4) principles are interlinked and must work together to achieve synergy.

Just as in synergy, where the whole is greater than the sum of its parts, so it is with these quadrants together with all the other Biblical principles this book is teaching you.

Quadrant One: Be Fruitful

And God blessed them and said unto them, ***be fruitful***. This is the first command of God and like stated above, we obey a King's command. To be fruitful simply means to *be productive, get results and be fertile*.

In his book**, "***Be all you can be***"**, author **John Maxwell** defines *"fruitfulness as a state of being active and showing positive attitudes on daily basis in our lives. This he said produces five "PRs" in our lives such as Positive Results, Positive Reactions, Positive Reinforcement, and Positive Rejoicing because of applying Right Principles."* The question to you *is how fruitful have you been in your life so far?*

To understand this principle of fruitfulness, one must understand that it is a worldwide truth that I cannot bear fruit without first sowing a seed. So the question is *where is the seed to obey this command from the King?* To understand this question, let us go back to Genesis where it all began and find solutions from the mind of the Creator.

> *And God said let the earth bring forth grass, the herb yielding seed, and the fruit tree yielding fruit after his kind, whose seed is in itself, upon the earth: and it was so. 12And the earth brought forth grass and herb yielding seed after his kind, and the tree yielding fruit, whose seed was in itself, after his kind: and God saw that it was good.* **Genesis 1:11-12 (KJV)**

The Seed Principle. (Two key Sources)

1. The spoken Word

In this verse you discover that God began by speaking a word, *let the earth bring forth grass, herbs and fruit trees* and it happened exactly as He said. The spoken word of God here should not be taken for granted as mere words. *"Now the parable is this: The seed is the word of God."* **Luke 8:11.** So, as God spoke to the earth to bring forth results, He actually impregnated it to yield results.

In the same light, because you have been created in His image, the words you speak also have creative powers. The words of your lips are also *quick and powerful, sharper than any double-edged sword especially when such words are based on God's Word.*

2. Self-seed

Everything God has created already has a *seed in itself.* This explains why most fruits you pick will usually have a seed in it, which can be planted to get more fruits. This is so with every living thing, including you. In verse 24 of Genesis 1, you can confirm that God used this same principle to create not only grass and herbs but all kinds of animals, livestock and humans.

This is the main reason why God did not command human to be *seedful but fruitful,* because everything around you is a seed and it remains your responsibility to become fruitful, replenish, subdue and multiply. Bill Gates, Steve Jobs, etc. are all men who have become fruitful with what they have. It does not matter whether you are a believer or not, this principle is for all. *The seed is your gifts, abilities, ideas, intelligence to write or even start a business and more.*

"For God is the one who gives seed to the farmer and then bread to eat. In the same way, he will give you many opportunities to do good, and he will produce a great harvest of generosity in you." **2 Cor. 9:10 (NLT)**

God is the **seed giver**, you are the farmer and what you do with your seed determines whether you will gain more fruits or not. Your gifts both spiritual and physical, talents, passion, potentials and purpose are what we are talking about here.

> Everything God has created already has a *seed in itself.*

God gives you seeds not just to eat but as a farmer you do business with your seed and then get bread to eat. God never intended man to be seed eaters but sowers because you never become fruitful by eating your seed.

A **seed sower** is one who does something with what God has given him. For instance, you have a gift or an idea and you follow up that idea or gift to bless people and become fruitful. In a nutshell, any person who adds value to what he already has is a seed sower. This is what fruitfulness means in relation to honouring God.

A **seed eater** is one who does nothing with what he has. It may be a gift, passion, an idea or more. He is just like a farmer who destroys all his seed before harvest. When you have a brilliant idea which can fetch you millions of money and you do not follow up with it, you are considered a seed eater and this dishonours God. Imagine if Steve Jobs of Apple Mac had eaten his idea. *What do you think would have happened in this generation when it comes to technology?*

Be results-oriented

God is interested in everything you do. He is constantly seeking results. Every seed God has given you will be accounted for on the judgment day, for *"it is appointed for man to live once after that judgement."* **Hebrews 9:27.**

There is a story in the Word of God that explains to us how results-oriented God is when it comes to man becoming fruitful and productive.

> *"Now listen to this story. A certain landowner planted a vineyard, built a wall around it, dug a pit for pressing out the grape juice, and built a lookout tower. Then he leased the vineyard to tenant farmers and moved to another country. 34At the time of the grape harvest he sent his servants to collect his share of the crop. 35But the farmers grabbed his servants, beat one, killed one, and stoned another.* **Matthew 21:33-35 (NLT)**

> When God wants to judge you, He seeks for results.

In this story, there are at least 5 things we can learn from our Creator.

1. God is the Landowner.

Not only is He the seed giver, He owns everything as well. Remember He is the source of life. Whether an entrepreneur, business owner or preacher, recognise Him as the owner of all life sources and you will be blessed.

2. God makes everything available for man to be fruitful.

V. 43 again teach us how the landowner planted the vineyard, built a wall around it, dug a pit for pressing out the grapes juice and built a lookout tower. This simply means that everything you need to succeed has already been provided by God. All you need is discover your seed and use it well.

3. You are a steward of everything you have:

Again in verse 33, the landowner (God) leased the vineyard to farmers (mankind). To lease is to *grant temporary possession or use to another for a specific period of time*.

This is why everything you have is not completely yours. Man is a caretaker of everything God has given Him, including all gifts and talents, ideas, even your husband, wife, siblings, life and more. Remember in *the kingdom of God, man has access to everything but owns nothing*.

4. When God wants to judge you, He seeks for results.

You will notice in v.34 in this story how at the time of harvest, the owner sent servants to collect his share. This is exactly what God will do to you. At judgment day, He will ask the question, *what did you do with what I leased to you?*

This is a question of maximising your potentials and abilities. Not only once or twice in this story did the owner seek for results; meaning God is constantly seeking for results. Beloved, this is the heart beat of God, that we become fruitful, multiply, subdue and replenish.

5. The world will pay you for your fruitfulness.

Not only is God interested in your fruitfulness, the whole world is waiting for your manifestation. By your fruits, you shall be known, and that also includes your manifested ideas, businesses and inventions.

Today the world is paying for the works of Bill Gates and Steve Jobs and the likes. *Why not you?* Have you thought about this? Well, if you have not, then you have got to start thinking about this now, because the same power of dominion also resides in you.

> It is easy to operate in life as a tree with many leaves but no fruits.

Fruitfulness begins with identifying the problems close to you and solving them. The world will not pay you for your skills, experience or exposure that is not harnessed for; people will pay you for the solving problems. Do you know that:

Halle Berry earns $30 a minute because of who she is?

Tiger Woods earns $175 a minute because of what he does?

Steven Spielberg earns $675 a minute because of what he has others doing?

Bill Gates earns $6,750 a minute because of what he has the world doing?

These are men you and I are paying for their fruitfulness. Fruitfulness is connected to who you are, what you do, what you get others doing and what you get the world to do.

Never be only full of leaves

It is easy to operate in life as a tree with many leaves but no fruits. What do I mean? We have a lot of promising people in the world today yet without results; fruitful in appearance yet physically and spiritually barren. **Mark 11:12-15** explains to us how Jesus cursed a fig tree just because it had more leaves but no fruits.

Precious one, it is not enough to be promising, do not just be an ideologist or somebody noted for talking about things. Do not waste precious time or space and still produce nothing. Everything about you is meant to be productive. Your lack of productivity will not be tolerated forever, so begin today and do something with what you have. It is in the place of doing things that God delights in us. God expects you to be fruitful to the point that any man that refuses to bear fruit shall be cut off actually.

"I am the true vine, and my Father is the gardener. 2He cuts off every branch that doesn't produce fruit, and he prunes the branches that do bear fruit so they will produce even more. ***John 15:1-2 (NLT)***

"Then Jesus used this illustration: "A man planted a fig tree in his garden and came again and again to see if there was any fruit on it, but he was always disappointed. 7Finally, he said to his gardener, 'I've waited three years, and there hasn't been a single fig! Cut it down. It's taking up space we can use for something else.'

8"The gardener answered, 'Give it one more chance. Leave it another year, and I'll give it special attention and plenty of fertilizer. 9If we get figs next year, fine. If not, you can cut it down.' ***"Luke 13:6-9 (NLT)***

*So every tree that does not produce good fruit is chopped down and thrown into the fire. **Matthew 7:19 (NLT)***

All these scriptures have one thing in common. God expects you to maximise your abilities, do something with what you have, apply His word to your life to affect families and the world we live in. He demands all mankind to be result-oriented, purpose-driven, seeking knowledge, getting understanding and applying wisdom in careers, business, gifts and talents.

> It is in the place of doing things that God delights in us.

Why? Because this is who He is and does and since you are in His image, you have been pre destined to conform to His likeness. Anything short of this disqualifies you to be called the image of His divine likeness.

Areas of fruitfulness.

When God commanded man to be fruitful (productive, yielding results), he meant this in every area of man's life. Therefore, His delegated authority should not be underestimated to one specific area or people or even a nation. From the social or political environment to every creature on this planet, man possesses the capacity to rule and make impact.

> It is a mistake for man to think that God's dominion mandate to him is only to populate the earth.

This is why it is a mistake for man to think that God's dominion mandate to him is only to populate the earth. Having children is not the only way to productivity. Today some traditions still place a lot of emphasis on having children and if after six months to a year a marriage is without procreation, family members begin to ask threatening questions and raise eyebrows. Even in some instances in certain cultures, having only female children without a male child also can become a big issue.

Admittedly, having children constitutes fruitfulness and I pray God blesses every couple with children, but this mandate involves more than just having children, every aspect of your life must bear fruits. Here is what I mean.

1. Fruit of your lips.

God expects even the words which come out of your mouth to bear fruits. Just as God spoke to bring the earth into being, the words of your mouth have the capacity to create good or evil. There is no movement in the valley of dry bones until God's word is uttered.

> *A man's belly shall be satisfied with the fruit of his mouth; and with the increase of his lips shall he be filled.* ***Proverbs 18:20 (KJV)***

> *By him therefore let us offer the sacrifice of praise to God continually, that is, the fruit of our lips giving thanks to his name.* ***Hebrews 13:15 (KJV)***

2. Fruit of your labour / work:

This refers to whatever your hands find doing. If you do your work well, you shall get results.

> **You will enjoy the fruit of your labour. How happy you will be! How rich your life! Psalm 128:2 (NLT)**

3. Fruit of the Spirit:

This is the expression of the Person of Christ, Who is the inward nature of those who believe. The Holy Spirit in a person produces this kind of fruits. God is not only interested in the outside manifestation of yielding results. The holistic nature of this principle also includes your inward spiritual life, for it is even the spiritual that controls the physical.

But the fruit of the Spirit is love, joy, peace, longsuffering, gentleness, goodness, faith, 23Meekness, temperance: against such there is no law. **Galatians 5:22-23 (KJV)**

Let us examine these fruits below:
- **Love:** God's *unconditional love* characterized by *self-sacrifice.*
- **Joy:** God's joy *not based on material things* but on *spiritual blessings.*
- **Peace:** the *tranquility* based on *God's sovereign love* and *acceptance.*
- **Longsuffering:** *enduring unfair treatment* by other people, as Christ did.
- **Gentleness:** treating others with the same kindness *God has shown us.*
- **Goodness:** expressing the *moral purity* and *righteousness* of God.
- **Faithfulness:** being as *trustworthy* as God.
- **Meekness:** displaying *God's humility* in our dealing with others.

❖ **Self-Control:** experiencing *God's control* over our fleshly desires.

These are all areas to apply this principle to be fruitful.

Principles and Promises

Every man can apply these **principles** in life and be fruitful; however, there is a deeper level to man's dominion mandate. Remember how God yearns to have a relationship with you? Our potential for bearing fruit is greater when connected to Jesus as our source.

It is our partnership with Jesus that ensures tremendous fruits in our lives more than we ourselves trying on our own. Again, our partnership with God moves us beyond **principles** into His divine **Promise**. Our dominion mandate first is a principle and secondly a promise.

> Our dominion mandate first is a principle and secondly a promise.

The principle nature of our dominion mandate means that anyone who works hard will achieve a level of fruitfulness, multiplication, replenishment and subduing. However, it is a promise for those who build relationship with Jesus and obey God's commandments. This releases and builds God's purpose in our lives.

> [12] *The righteous shall flourish like the palm tree: he shall grow like a cedar in Lebanon.* [13] *Those that be planted in the house of the Lord shall flourish in the courts of our God.* [14] *They shall still bring forth fruit in old age; they shall be fat and flourishing;* **Psalm 92:12-14 (KJV)**

In this scripture God is talking to the righteous (those in right standing with God) and those planted in His house and promises to cause them to flourish and bear fruit even in old age. This is something that goes beyond general principle.

In John 15, Jesus gives us a three-way formula for fruitfulness. This formula is a promise, not a principle, for those who choose to:
1. **Remain / abide in Him**
2. **Receive**
3. **Reproduce.**

However, it is not enough to only be fruitful. After discovering your seed and sowing it to yield fruits, your fruits must be multiplied to make impact.

Quadrant Two: Multiply.

The second commandment from God after being fruitful is to *multiply;* meaning that man must not only focus on becoming fruitful but also seek to *multiply fruits*. This means that, your first step to dominion is *fruit bearing* after which you must pursue *fruit multiplication*. I therefore sincerely believe that the second most important question we must all ask ourselves after every victory (fruitfulness) is *what we can do to multiply such victories (fruits)?*.

Whenever you become fruitful in life but fail to go to the next level, it is only a matter of time before your fruits fade away. Majority of people in this category are failing or have failed just because they failed to multiply their fruits.

Let me break it down this way. *As an author, I consider myself being fruitful when I have written a book. But I must ask myself whether it is enough just to produce one copy of the book to myself.*

The answer is emphatically NO. To really take charge and control of the market, I must begin to think of multiplying the book so I can dominate the market as I make it available on a larger scale to others.

> Whenever you become fruitful in life but fail to go to the next level, it is only a matter of time before your fruits fade away.

This is the principle of multiplication and this simple illustration can be applied to everything you can think of. Imagine if Steve Jobs had produced Apple for himself alone or Mary Kay had manufactured her brand of products and been satisfied with using it by herself. This is why after your fruits, you must think multiplication.

What therefore is to multiply? To multiply is simply *to increase* in your potential. God has created in all of us the ability to grow, expand and maximise. The first point of doing this is by being fruitful and all of us have the capacity to be fruitful. All we need to do is to discover our seed and sow it.

Secondly, to *multiply is a mathematical operation of scaling one number over the other.* As God is interested in multiplying, so should

> Your ability to multiply is to think options, opportunities, and many doors instead of one.

you because you were made in His image. This is why before Him, one may slay a thousand but two may slay not two thousand but ten thousand.

Again, the word multiply consists of two words, which are '**multi**' and '**ply**'. *Multi simply means many or more than two*, meaning your ability to multiply is to think options, opportunities, and many doors instead of one. The key to walking in dominion starts from affecting many lives with your fruits or productivity so if you are not affecting the world with your degrees, inventions, creativity or more, then you are not walking in dominion. Instead of being fenced in, rather be driven by the desire and passion to increase your potential and capacity.

To ply is to practice or perform diligently; meaning that multiplying my fruits involves hard work and constant persistence. You must seek to ply your gift, talent, discovery to many people beyond yourself. Ply also comes from the Latin word **plicare** which means *to fold the layers of a multi-layer material such as plywood*. Another key to walking in dominion is to understand the structural nature of life.

What God is teaching mankind from His most important mandate to man is that life works effectively in layers. All the four quadrants (fruitfulness, multiplication, replenishing, subduing) together with all the principles this book offers represent the layers which, when culminated or sown together, will cause you to walk in dominion.

How to Multiply Fruits

Now that we have an understanding of what God means to multiply, do you desire to expand, grow, maximise your gifts, think many doors and opportunities? Yes I believe you do. Begin by transforming your mind from *I Cannot? Can I? to How can I?*

1. Have fruits:

Never think to multiply until you have fruits. So if you have nothing to show forth, get back to the beginning of this chapter and sow your seeds to reap your fruits. Stop saying *I cannot* be fruitful or stop asking the question, *can I* be fruitful? Start asking *how can I* bear fruit?

2. Prayer

The truth is, you cannot do without prayer. Any man who refuses to practice the discipline and lifestyle of prayer is only hindering himself from progress. As established firmly throughout creation, God is the source of everything. Whatever you seek to multiply, first pray to Him for wisdom and guidance, for no one works in multiplication except through Him?

It was the great reformer Martin Luther who said, *"I have much to do today, I will need to spend another hour on my knees"* To him, prayer was a foundation of power in releasing and multiplying his efforts.

> You are going nowhere with what you have if you are not willing to get people involved.

He understood that if he did not practice diligence to prayer, he will become a prey and stray from the right path.

The idea is to get God to be our source of energy, to refresh, renew and help recommit us to His original plan, which involves multiplying our efforts. This is why prayer is important for everyone. The question therefore is not *can I pray?* Or **I cannot pray**? But *How can I pray?*

3. Build right connections.

While fruitfulness usually depends on you, multiplying your fruits must include people. Again, as an author, my manuscript is my fruit and it mainly depends on me to get it out of myself (seed). However, to get out to the market, I need people to make this happen. You are going nowhere with what you have if you are not willing to get people involved. You must be prepared to work together with others, for it will take more than you to multiply your business, ministry, etc.

Quadrant Three: Replenish

The third quadrant in God's first commandment to man is to replenish. Before we even delve deeper into what God means by replenish, there are a number of false concepts relating to the Genesis account of creation. Among those is the currently popular "**Gap Theory**," which is also known as **'Ruin-Reconstruction theory'** by Scottish theologian **Thomas Chalmers.**

He (Thomas) suggests that a pre-Adamic race had perished as a result of a so-called 'Lucifer's flood' and so what God meant was to re-fill the gap the pre-Adamic world and race had created. This theory is fallacious and wrong because of three main reasons my Spirit leads me to pour to you.

1. The Hebrew meaning of replenish is to fill and not to re-fill.
2. Biblically, Paul inspired by the Holy Ghost in **1 Corinthians 15:45-48**, stated categorically that "the first man, Adam became a living person..." This establishes Adam as the first man to be created by God and there was not any pre-Adamic race or world.
3. As established, I personally view this commandment from God as quadrants that do not only constitute having children or populating the world alone. The four things God commanded also are principles that have the capacity of affecting your business, ministry and everything.

As explained in this chapter, first you must yield the fruits which are as a direct result of the seed God has already planted in you even before this commandment. Then must follow multiplying your fruits before you replenish.

To replenish therefore means *the ability to ensure that God's given seed (talents, passion), which has resulted into multiplied fruits, continues to perpetuate without fail. As multiplication breeds the increase, replenishment of your business, talents, ideas, and gifts enables constancy and permanence.*

The purpose of replenishment is to ensure two main things, *continuity* and *sustainability*. To ensure that your books, music album, ministry or business stays on the market for instance, you must work hard at it. Even though to replenish depends on God, you have a major part to play. God is the seed giver to your fruits; He helps you to multiply, but to ensure continuity and sustainability (replenish), you must provide the ingredients.

Author and Pastor Norman Vincent Peale said "Ask the God who made you to keep remaking you."

Quadrant Four: Subdue

The fourth quadrant in God's most important commandment to man is to subdue the earth and this is very important. The process of walking in dominion is never complete without subduing. You can be fruitful, multiply and replenish, but when you fail to subdue your fears, enemies or even competition, you are then bound to fail.

To subdue is *to conquer, overcome or bring under control by either physical or spiritual force.* God knows from the beginning that there will be battles and challenges on your way to dominion. Few people, business and companies make it to this level but everyone has the potential to get there.

It takes a lot of resilience, commitment and consistency to move up this level. The purpose of this quadrant is to ensure that as you become successful, you do not slack off at the moments of walking in complete dominion. This is why God has placed in this quadrant, things that you have to overcome to maintain your sense of balance of success.

The principle of 'subdue' also determines the legacy you will leave behind. Everyone is born with a legacy, a potential to become great, but we all determine the legacy we will leave behind. It is what we leave behind that will determine the platform, even for the next generation.

Perhaps the biggest question we all need to ask ourselves is '***what do you want to be said of you or leave behind when you are no more one day?***' whether you will be great or not is determined by this question. The good thing is that, you do not have to be dead before you live it. It begins now.

Whereas the first three quadrants lay emphasis on God's already endowed abilities inside of you from birth, this last quadrant purely depends on God's own weapons and strength. Why, you may ask? Because it is at the very top of your success that the enemy will arise against what you have struggled to build.

In other words, the first three quadrants are in built within your genetic blueprint whiles quadrant four is outside of you. The problem with the world system is in how we define greatness. Many in this world define greatness as material wealth, fame, power and high social status but this is not entirely true. These maybe the result of greatness but not entirely the heart of greatness.

The most successful and great people are those who builds and impact people. **Myles Munroe** rightly said it in his book (Pass It On) that greatness is measured by the transfer of success to future generation. This is the principle the fourth quadrant depicts. In his book, *from Good to Great*, author **Jim Collins,** for fifteen years put together a research team of twenty one people to find out what makes some companies move from good to great and from great to failure.

The major element in Collins' book, as I deduce, is not about economic hardship or even the arrival of new technologies in the world, but the main point is how the truth still remains about maintaining relevance and impacting the next generation irrespective of who you are or the company you own. These are principles that should never change if you or your company or ministry will move from good to great.

You can be good and even move to be great and yet fall back to grass if you do not heed to some of these principles this book throws light on. It is also a true fact at this level of your success that ignoring the author and finisher of life can move you back in the order of the quadrants.

To fulfill quadrant four, you must be fully prepared, stand on your ground, seek and show godly wisdom to every force and opposition against your progress.

Three (3) key powers that are difficult to conquer are **self, sin and Satan.** Nobody achieves significance on this earth without overcoming challenges of various sorts. It will take faith, strength and a covenant with God through the Holy Spirit's ability to completely walk in dominion.

In this quadrant, we focus on these three issues above; those powers that try to conquer us and what we need to conquer such things.

Powers that seek to conquer us (3s)

1. Self:

Many at times, the cause of our failure in business, ministry, and ideas should not be attributed to anyone but us. We can be our own worst enemies by even walking ourselves out of our own destinies. First learn to subdue your inward self before your outer demons. If we fail to conquer self, self-conquers us, as private victories precede public victories.

> First learn to subdue your inward self before your outer demons.

You cannot seek to improve your circumstance and yet be unwilling to self-crucify your flesh. This is true of earthly and heavenly things. Every one of us must be willing to read more, think more, work more and train more, but this is what human nature dislikes.

The good is usually the enemy to greatness. You can be satisfied with just being fruitful and never make it to greatness. It is negative attitudes, lack of self-control, discipline and determination, which always stop us from completing our walk into dominion. One Biblical character is **Samson**. This man Samson had the complete package yet failed to subdue his own fleshly desires. Samson is like a modern day man who also has the fruits, multiplies and replenishes his fruits but lack of self-control and motivation causes him to lose it all.

2. Sin:

Today, there is no doubt that sin has entered the world and we are experiencing its effect. It is anything that displeases God or always *Simple Instructions Neglected*. When you neglect to do what needs to be done, you are bound to fail. This is one major area the world system is failing to conquer, as the system has become weaker by the clock. The effect of neglecting God's simple instructions is what our generation is currently experiencing.

Sin does not only weaken a person or nation, it dulls it too. It takes away the power to walk in dominion. The man or nation that sins lacks power and sin has the capacity to dethrone us from reaching the top. Sin permits enemy forces to lock you out of business, ministry and everything you can think of. Why? Because Satan thrives on it as God looks away. Read **Hebrews 12: 1, Ephesians 5:3-5** for more emphasis.

In the book of **Joshua, Chapter 7,** the nation Israel failed to subdue the land of Ai. Prior to this, they had been fruitful and even multiplied their victory over stronger nations. Yet when it came to subduing a smaller nation like Ai, they failed. Why? The answer is in verse 1 of chapter 7. A man named Achan had neglected simple instructions from the LORD. It was not until they dealt with that sin that they could overcome that nation.

> Anything that takes away your joy, progress, peace and your complete walk into dominion has a satanic source

In the same light, if you are to completely walk in kingdom dominion, you and I together with our leaders and nations must deal with sin, desist neglecting simple instructions and principles laid down as the ancient landmarks.

3. Satan:

Anything that takes away your joy, progress, peace and your complete walk into dominion has a satanic source and you must begin to pray now. Your number one adversary is Satan who *comes to steal, kill and destroy*. You must always lift up the Almightiness of God against every might of Satan in your life.

Be careful of negative ideas, thoughts and suggestions about your business and most importantly your walk and relationship with God. Giants of the faith, leaders of society and nobles have all fallen prey to Satan's tactics. This can happen to you when you allow Satan to dethrone the better knowledge of the power of God for you.

So you must be careful of his evil schemes, so that Satan does not outsmart you, especially in these last days. Satan is currently destroying man with fear, frustration and defeated mentality. Worry is a root cause of all manners of sickness in today's generation. Depression, stress, etc. are all as a result of doubt.

What you need to subdue.

The rest of the chapters in this book are all based on the *four key quadrants* in this chapter. As you read on, you will discover what it takes to fulfill the quadrants and what you need to move from one level to the other.

APPLYING YOUR DOMINION MANDATE TO YOUR LIFE

1. Understand that the source of your authority spurns from the fact that you were created in the image of God and that you were wired in your DNA to be fruitful, multiply, replenish and subdue.

2. Everything in life is a seed. Begin from today to implement right positive attitude on daily basis. Like John Maxwell said, you will attract **Positive Results, Positive Reactions, Positive Reinforcement, and Positive Rejoicing** because of applying Right Principles.

3. In what ways have you positioned yourself so that the world will pay for your fruitfulness? Begin today by defining:
   ❖ Who are you (**fruits**)?
   ❖ What do you do (**multiply**)?
   ❖ What have you got others to do (**replenish**)?
   ❖ What have you got the world to do (**subdue**)?

4. The mandate of fruitfulness goes beyond only having children. To walk in kingdom dominion considers the many areas mentioned in this chapter and expands your productivity in life.

5. In moving from fruit production to fruit multiplications consider ways you can improve, expand and maximize what you have.

6. How do you deal with the three most important powers that stop man from achieving at the fourth quadrant of 'subdue': **sin, self, Satan**?

7. Shift your thinking from 'I can't? Can I?' to How can I?

8. Are you connected to the right business, ministry partners? Decide for yourself whether it is time to drop friends who cannot take you to the highest quadrant and connect to the right ones.
9. Think of the kind of legacy you want to leave behind? How do you want your family, friends, or even society to remember you one day when you are no more? It begins today so do something about it.

QUADRANT I

THE POWER OF KNOWING YOURSELF

Know yourself to grow yourself

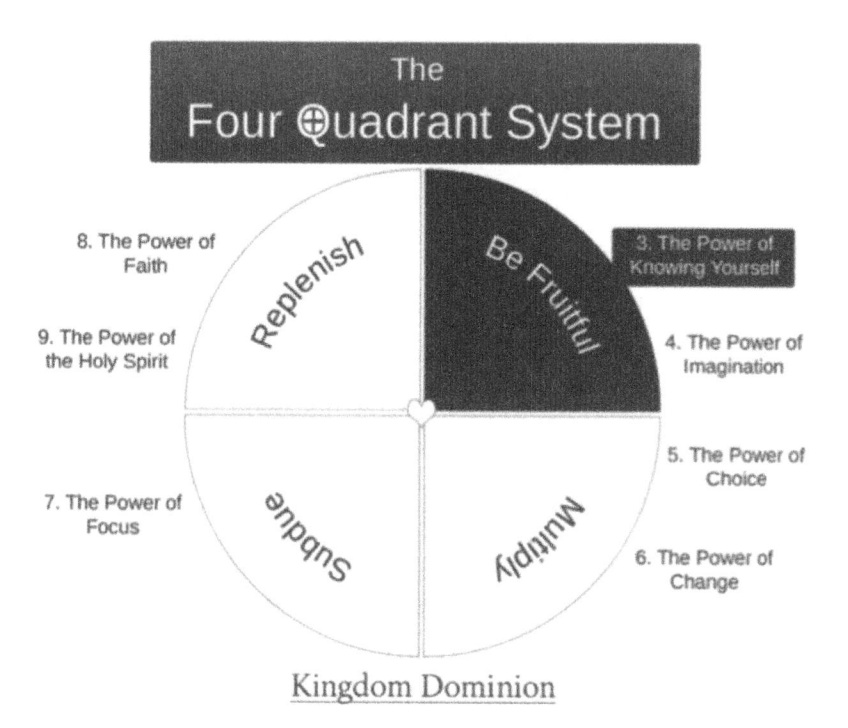

The Four Quadrant System

- 3. The Power of Knowing Yourself
- 4. The Power of Imagination
- 5. The Power of Choice
- 6. The Power of Change
- 7. The Power of Focus
- 8. The Power of Faith
- 9. The Power of the Holy Spirit

Replenish · Be Fruitful · Multiply · Subdue

Kingdom Dominion

3

THE POWER OF KNOWING YOURSELF/AWARENESS ABILITY

For you to fulfill quadrant one (fruitfulness), you must first be aware of yourself. There is a tremendous power in getting to know you. No human can become somebody until he recognises the unique abilities the Creator has deposited in him. **Anwar Sadat**, past President of Egypt once said, *real success is success with self. It is not having things, but in having mastery, having victory over self.* Indeed, one area you must think of improving is the area of self. Instead of focusing on changing others, we must first think of changing ourselves, because the toughest person to lead is always you.

If we are honest with ourselves, you will admit that we see others different from the way we see ourselves. We tend to judge people by their actions while we give room to our intentions. Most of the times, the enemy is not Satan but us. This problem usually occurs because we neglect this all-important ability of self-awareness and try to shift the blame to others. *"The soul that has no established aim loses itself."* **Michel de Montaigne**

This significantly limits our level of fruitfulness, potential and our ability to relate to others effectively. But as we begin to know ourselves: strength and weakness, interest and opportunities, it begins to generate the seed necessary to grow and beget fruitfulness. This is the reason why man has been mandated to have dominion over all things and why we can progress through the process of fruitfulness to multiplication to replenishment and to subduing. Animals do not possess this ability.

For there to be a fruit, there must first be a seed, so in actual fact, God should have commanded man to rather be "**seedful**". But no, we are commanded to be "**fruitful**". This means that inside every created human being lays a ready-made seed which must be located and maximised (fruitful). *Your ability to locate your seed and be fruitful with it is what constitutes self-awareness.*

It is also one's ability to identify potentials and take responsibility to be productive with it. It is amazing how many people blame God for their failures in life today. Individuals and even nations even have swayed from the truth and no longer believe in God. It will startle you to know that most of the things we blame Him for are actually His expectation for us to solve.

Self-awareness also is being conscious that you have some decisions and choices to make in life and that God is simply there to guide and support you, but then you have a major part to play.

Knowing yourself and identifying your capabilities will help you to live

> In life, what you have but do not see is always greater than what you have and can see.

effectively and also empower you to be all you were created to be. Admittedly, we may be limited from creation, but when we discover our self-abilities, we push back the boundaries of our limitations.

The Four Quadrants To Greatness.

The key difference between this ability of self-discovery and your imagination is that, whilst your imagination allows you to create the future and envision your potential, knowing yourself will help you to live the future you have already created in your mind.

> No human can become somebody until he recognises the unique abilities the Creator has deposited in him.

Self-awareness calls for knowing both your strength and weakness but making a choice to work and operate from your strength. When you know your strength and capabilities and choose to work in them, you allow what you possess to empower you.

On the other hand, when you do not know yourself and operate in your weakness, you activate what you do not possess to empower you. The Biblical story in **Acts 3:1-7 (KJV)** speaks very clearly about knowing who you are, what you can do and separating your strength from your weakness.

> *"Now Peter and John went up together into the temple at the hour of prayer, being the ninth hour. 2And a certain man lame from his mother's womb was carried, whom they laid daily at the gate of the temple which is called Beautiful, to ask alms of them that entered into the temple; 3Who seeing Peter and John about to go into the temple asked an alms. 4And Peter, fastening his eyes upon him with John, said, Look on us. 5And he gave heed unto them, expecting to receive something of them. 6Then Peter said, Silver and gold have I none; but such as I have give I thee: In the name of Jesus Christ of Nazareth rise up and walk. 7And he took him by the right hand, and lifted him up: and immediately his feet and ancle bones received strength."*

In this story lie key principles about the power of self-awareness.

a) **Know what you do not have in life.**

These two men *knew what they did not possess*, that was silver and gold (money).

b) **Be fully aware of what you have.**

It is very evident in the story that though they did not have silver and gold (money), they recognized what they had, so out of what they had, they gave the lame man something money could not buy, the power to walk again.

c) Another observation I want to bring your attention to is the statement that, **in life, what you have but do not see is always greater than what you have and can see.**

"Now glory be to God! By his mighty power at work within us, he is able to accomplish infinitely more than we would ever dare to ask or hope." **Ephesians. 3:20 (NLT)**

Notice that the lame man had always received money from different people but had never received the kind of healing he needed, but on that fateful day when Peter and John passed by, though they did not have physical money, they gave him what was greater than money, which was breaking him free from bondage.

You may not have physical things, but believe me, there are things God has deposited in you and if only you can become aware of these specific spiritual and physical gifts, you will discover that there is no limit to possibilities in your life and destiny. This is how powerfully this principle of self-discovery can function in your life.

Dangers of Lack of Self-Awareness

One day, after God had fully prepared Moses for 40 years in the wilderness, He appeared to him and asked him to go and deliver His people (Israelites) from slavery, but Moses refused and

> What do you have in your hands?
> Who needs what I have?
> What can I do with what I have?

protested. Like most of us, we forget that after God has fully prepared us in life for a task, He will appear to us.

But Moses protested again, "Look, they won't believe me! They won't do what I tell them. They'll just say, 'The LORD never appeared to you.' 2Then the LORD asked him, "What do you have there in your hand?" A shepherd's staff," Moses replied."Throw it down on the ground," the LORD told him. So Moses threw it down, and it became a snake! Moses was terrified, so he turned and ran away. 4Then the LORD told him, "Take hold of its tail." So Moses reached out and grabbed it, and it became a shepherd's staff again. **Exodus 4:1-4 (NLT)**

Moses' main problem was that he was ignorant of himself. He lacked self-awareness and this can cause untold damage in our lives, especially to our gifts and productivity. We see these characteristics in Moses' life at this point and the same can be said of those who exhibit similar character. Below are some of the dangers of being ignorant of what you have.

1. **Fear:** I recently read an article on the fears that prevent people from walking in dominion. The following five fear factors are key as we not only look at Moses but you.
   - **Fear of failure**

- **Fear of trading security for the unknown**
- **Fear of being overextended financially**
- **Fear of what others will say or think**
- **Fear that success will alienate peers.**

Which of these reflects in your life? For me the first two are what I constantly deal with to enable me to win. The truth is we all have fear but we can deal with it by having faith. Like Smith Wigglesworth said, *"we can all move from the street called fear into Faith Victory Street."*

2. **Low self-esteem.** He underestimated himself.
3. **Reactive mindset:** He only saw weakness in his speech and that began to affect everything about him. Reactive people are always affected by their physical environment
4. **He activated the negative to empower him.**
5. **Ignorance.**

Do you know that the word **ignorant** in the Hebrew language means darkness and the ruler of all darkness in the world is Satan? This simply means that Satan rules in every area of ignorance in your life. His main purpose is to steal, kill and destroy (John 10:10).

But notice as God began to deal with him, He asked him one of the greatest questions in life, **what do you have in your hand**? To me this is one of the questions that can break the spirit of ignorance in your life.

In his hands was a stick he had been carrying for years but never was aware could become a useful tool for what God was preparing him for. I encourage you to read the full story of Moses and how he delivered the people from slavery and you will discover that it was his staff that God used to do mighty miracles before their enemies, such as even opening up the Red Sea.

As we shift attention back to you, I want you to understand that no man is hopeless as you sometimes think. God's question to Moses is also to you.

What do you have in your hands?

We all have something in life. In Moses' hands was just a stick; in yours might be a pen, voice, ideas, etc. It is your responsibility to identify it, no matter how small you think it may be.

Who needs what I have?

God always gives you something others need. In Moses' case, the Israelites needed deliverance. A whole generation is waiting for your impartation so your playing small will not help. Remember the world is ready to pay for your fruitfulness.

What can I do with what I have?

It is not until you start asking very important questions about yourself before you begin to be productive with what you have. Every question is a seed for a solution, that's why the more intelligent questions you ask the quicker you come out of fear, intimidation and ignorance. Moses' encounter with God demonstrated to him that he could actually do several things with what he had.

> God will always use what you have to give you what you need.

Indeed, not only did he turn the stick into a snake, he used it to turn water into blood, to command frogs to appear and to do a host of other things. In this same way, your encounter with God will empower you to know what you can do with what you have.

Sometimes people are aware of what they have only to think that it's not enough.

Is this not true? Have you not come in contact with people who think what they have is simply not enough to achieve greatness? Such people are always looking for more rather than dealing with self. This is why many people usually treat their gifts and talents as hobbies instead of making it the real deal.

Jesus' encounter with the five thousand people gives us a vivid example of this. One day, after the teacher had taught the people the Kingdom message, His disciples advised Him to send the people away to get something to eat. For what happened, join me

Mark 6:37-41 (NLT)

"But Jesus said, "You feed them." "With what?" they asked. "It would take a small fortune to buy food for all this crowd!" 38"How much food do you have?" he asked. "Go and find out." They came back and reported, "We have five loaves of bread and two fish." 39Then Jesus told the crowd to sit down in groups on the green grass. 40So they sat in groups of fifty or a hundred. 41Jesus took the five loaves and two fish, looked up toward heaven, and asked God's blessing on the food. Breaking the loaves into pieces, he kept giving the bread and fish to the disciples to give to the people."

To begin with, notice Jesus' answer to them, *"you feed them"*. In other words, He shifted responsibility into their hands. As a matter of fact, Jesus was trying to get them to understand that they already had something that contains the capacity to feed the over five thousand people (seed).

While Jesus was focusing on what they had, they asked the question *"with what do we feed them?"* This is a question of ignorance. We all usually ask this question when we know what we have is insignificant compared to what we need.

Then Jesus answered them again to go and find out what they had. Once more He teaches them that we are completely responsible for finding out what we have because

I. We always have something.

II. God will always use what you have to give you what you need.

This is why you never have to show up before God with empty hands requesting for solutions He already has equipped you with. They came back with five loaves of bread and two fishes. To them, it was something but not enough to feed the many people.

This is where the supernatural begins to work for you. Jesus did what was impossible with man but possible with God. Never underestimate the little you have because once you first identify the little you have, God then will use it to reach beyond man's limitation.

Keys to Self-Awareness

1. Responsibility

I believe that by now, you have already identified this point as a key requirement to knowing yourself. One word that has been reoccurring in this chapter so far has been 'Responsibility'. The first thing to do if you are to discover this ability and power is to learn to take responsibility for yourself and your actions. There is no point playing the blame game all the time.

Until you take personal responsibility for your life, you will never become who you want to be. *"For we are each responsible for our own conduct"* **Galatians 6:5 (NLT)**. God has given us voluntary powers of self-awareness and discovery that on our own responsibility, we might use that to our own benefits.

A 25-year-old once said, *"our background and circumstance may have influenced who we are, but we are responsible for who we become."* How true this is. When we blame circumstances and conditions for our actions all the time, we never receive the ability to know ourselves to move forward. The painful child upbringing and negative conditions usually contain the keys to your breakthrough in life.

Taking responsibility for your life and actions constitutes **5 key principles** this book throws a deeper light on:

a) You must understand that your greatest ability in life is your Responsibility.

If you cannot or are not willing to take responsibility for yourself, then this book is not for you. Even God cannot help you if you are unwilling to learn to take responsibility for yourself and life. Neither is your mother, father, siblings or anybody for that matter responsible for who you become. So simply grow up, make life by first taking responsibility for who you are.

God has laid on you the responsibility of saving your own life; even when it comes to salvation, we need to take the responsibility of accepting that work of grace. If you do not, no one can take that responsibility for you.

b) To be responsible simply means, you are RESPONSE–ABLE.

Wherever there is a stimulus, there is also a response. Stimuli *are the various conditions and circumstances that affect us on daily basis.* Somebody will offend you, you may experience failure on your pathway to success; rejections and frustrations are all stimulus situa-

=====
Until you take personal responsibility for your life, you will never become who you want to be.
=====

tions. What we all do is that we choose our Responses in every instance. Therefore, whether rain or shine, people treat you well or not, you are well able to choose your response. A person who understands this always makes the best out of every situation.

When life throws at you bitter lemons, you possess the power to make a refreshing lemon juice out of it or sit down and remain bitter. As **Eleanor Roosevelt** said, *"No one can hurt you without your consent."* It is always in your power to choose your imagination, even in the midst of a situation of chains or imprisonment.

This ability is already inside you from the day you were born. This is why Jesus told His disciples to go back and find out what they had. All you need is to take charge of your life, activate this power and use it.

Life always features crisis periods. There are seasons in your life when things you do not like will happen to you. What being responsible does is it helps you to overcome crisis and outlast difficult seasons. When you follow the story of Joseph, one important thing you learn from this young man is his sense of responsibility in the midst of crisis.

No wonder God was always with him, helping him to overcome issues. God strengthens us and helps us when we first take responsibility in situations.

c) Your ABILITIES need RESPONSE to survive.

When you take the word 'Responsibility' into perspective, you also discover that you possess the ability to be fruitful in life and there is a reason (purpose) why God has built in you gifts and talents. That ability to write, sing, preach, start a Business, begin a project, influence lives, start a family, etc., demands a response. Unless you respond to your abilities in life, your purpose will never be fulfilled.

> God is the power over all powers and He can empower you to do what you normally cannot do.

No matter how brilliant, beautiful or friendly you may be, ideas remain ideas and thought always remain thought if not operated upon. The problem with most people is that of LOW SELF-ESTEEM. Most people with potential out there have the ability to be successful but lack the courage to move forward. This is why the first thing one need to do is to take Responsibility for one's actions, because Responsibility simply means you have ABILITY but you have just got to RESPOND to it.

If you are a Leader and you are reading this book, I encourage you to make room for people to exhibit their talents and gifts at work, home or even in the church

d) Your natural abilities need God's super responses to enable you fulfill your supernatural abilities.

This is a stronger and deeper requirement to the steps above. Yes, you have the potential to do things on your own, but there comes a time when man cannot do more than he can do and this is where the super becomes more necessary. This is the point where your life and situation need heaven's intervention. Everybody needs Jesus. He is the Source of the super to strengthen your natural abilities to fulfil supernatural things in your life.

So do not always rely on yourself. Get to know Him and learn to rely and call on Him in good times and bad. This super ability comes from the Holy Spirit, the third Person of the Trinity. Read the whole Chapter on the Holy Spirit to understand more.

> *"This is what the LORD says to Cyrus, his anointed one, whose right hand he will empower. Before him, mighty kings will be paralyzed with fear. Their fortress gates will be opened, never again to shut against him."* **Isaiah 45:1 (NLT)**

This is an example of what the super abilities of the Holy Spirit can do to your natural abilities. God is the power over all powers and He can empower you to do what you normally cannot do. Just as Philip Schaff in his book, *"Creeds of Christendom, with a History and Critical notes. Volume I"*. s**aid,** *"Ability and opportunity are the measure of responsibility and God requires no more from man than he empowers him to perform."*

> Taking responsibility for your actions is the way to releasing what you need to succeed.

An advantage of personal responsibility is that it leads to building your character, integrity and trust. It helps one to focus and complete an assignment. The results of taking responsibility even go beyond self-awareness and discovery, it earns others respect and confidence. An immense responsibility pertains to revival. Revival is simply bringing back from coma what was once alive. It may be you, family, nation or even a generation. That's why you need to stay committed to taking responsibility, first for your life and then for others in your care.

Let's focus our attention on an example from Genesis. It is the story of Joseph and his brothers. *Joseph was sold into slavery by his brothers but survived this ordeal and became the Prime Minister in Egypt when he explained the King's dream and saved Egypt from famine. In the midst of the famine season, his brothers came searching for food.*

Joseph first recognised his brothers but they could not, for they did not expect him to have survived. On one occasion, he requested for his brother Benjamin to be sent to him but Jacob their father did not comply to this because he did not want to lose him too.

For what led to his release (fruitfulness), let's focus on two of the brothers, Reuben and Judah, and their statements.

> *"And Reuben spake unto his father, saying, <u>Slay my two sons</u>, if I bring him not to thee: deliver him into my hand, and I will bring him to thee again. 38And he said, <u>My son shall not go down with you</u>; for his brother is dead, and he is left alone: if mischief befall him by the way in the which ye go, then shall ye bring down my gray hairs with sorrow to the grave"*. **Genesis 42:37-38 (KJV)**

You noticed that Reuben's statement did not release Benjamin to go with them. Now when Judah went forward to speak, something changed.

> *"Judah said to his father, "Send the boy with me, and we will be on our way. Otherwise we will all die of starvation—and not only we, but you and our little ones. ²<u>I personally guarantee his safety. You may hold me responsible if I don't bring</u>*

him back to you. Then let me bear the blame forever 10For we could have gone and returned twice by this time if you had let him come without delay."

11So their father, Jacob, finally said to them, "If it can't be avoided, then at least do this. Fill your bags with the best products of the land. Take them to the man as gifts—balm, honey, spices, myrrh, pistachio nuts, and almonds. 13.Then take your brother and go back to the man". **Genesis 43:8-11,13 (NLT)**

Now the question I want to ask you is, *what made Jacob release Benjamin at the end?*

It was a matter of personal responsibility from Judah. All the while, Jacob being wise was looking for someone he could trust and put confidence in. Reuben's statement was that of irresponsibility, because he offered his children to die in the event something happened, while Judah personally guaranteed Benjamin's safety with his own life. He was not going to put the blame on his children like his elder brother Reuben did, but on himself.

When Jacob sensed that statement of personal responsibility from Judah, he released Benjamin. In the same way, taking responsibility for our actions is the way of releasing what is needed to succeed.

Just like Jacob, God is looking for people He can trust and put confidence in, people of character and integrity, ready to tap into this power of self-awareness. He will fill your life with the best, give you gifts and release your Benjamin (fruitfulness).

2. Knowing Christ

The surest way to knowing yourself is by first knowing Jesus Christ. Now the question is, do you know Jesus? Because if you do not know Him, it is going to be difficult to find what you have and do something with it, just like most of you are experiencing right now.

Christ is the author and finisher of your faith. In fact, when you read John Gospel Chapter 1, He is God's best idea that was manifested on two legs for the sake of all mankind, yet He remains the most misunderstood person on earth. No wonder there is a lot of confusion in the world today. He himself knew this fact when He was in the world. This is why He once asked His disciple the most important question, *who do people say I am*? (**Matthew 16:13-14**).

> Knowing who Christ truly is will change your life forever.

The Buddhist thinks He is just a wise man. Hindus think He is one of their 6 million gods; Muslims see Him as a Prophet who failed, which is why Mohammed was sent to complete His work. Even the Atheist sees Him as a thing of our imagination created by man to deceive the masses. Do you now understand why Jesus still is asking that question, *who do people say I am*? The saddest of all these is that even some Christian denominations are also confused about who He is.

The name Christ means *"the anointed King"* meaning He could not be a prophet, messenger or one of the gods. A ***king*** takes no instruction from anybody, He rules His territory. The word ***Anointed*** is to be empowered to function. Therefore Christ is empowered to rule the world. The earth is His and the fullness thereof. He is the LORD, Owner of everything.

Knowing who He (God) is will change your life forever. The best way to know yourself and the things you possess is to know Him and repent (change) from your old thought of Him. This is why He is still asking the question, who do you say I am? Let people continue to ask and confuse themselves with the supremacy of His kingdom, but He is asking you a personal question now, who do you think I am?

Matthew 16:13-19 (NLT)

15Then he asked them, "Who do you say I am?" .16Simon Peter answered, "You are the Messiah, the Son of the living God." 17Jesus replied, "You are <u>blessed</u>, Simon son of John, because my Father in heaven has revealed this to you. You did not learn this from any human being. 18Now I say to you that you are Peter, and <u>upon this rock I will build my church</u>, and all the <u>powers of hell will not conquer it</u>. 19And I will give you <u>the keys of the Kingdom of Heaven</u>. Whatever you lock on earth will be locked in heaven, and whatever you open on earth will be opened in heaven."

Just like Simon Peter above, you must recognise Christ as the Messiah (saviour of your life), the Son of the living God. This is the first step to knowing yourself because He holds the keys to your life. The underlined verses above will become your portion.

When Peter understood who He was, Jesus blessed him. The word *bless* means happy. Secondly, He prophesied into his life His purpose for him when He said, *upon this rock I will build my church, and all the powers of hell will not conquer it.* Then He gave him keys to the Kingdom of Heaven, representing fundamental principles that will unlock every blessing in heaven and on earth.

This is what knowing Christ is all about. It is about you. This is *the law of Recognition.*

3. Listen and learn from successful people

Solomon, the wisest that has ever lived on the surface of the earth said in His book of **Ecclesiastes 1: 9-10 (NLT)**, that *"History merely repeats itself. It has all been done before. Nothing under the sun is truly new. What can you point to that is new? How do you know that it did not exist or it did not already exist long time ago"?*

I guess the lesson Solomon is teaching us here is very simple. Whatever you desire to achieve in life has already been accomplished by someone in one way or the other. Whether it is about becoming a millionaire, inventing a car, creating your own fashion line, writing a book, a song and more, always beware that there are and have already been pacesetters ahead of you. Things have happened in former times you can easily learn from.

This is why listening and learning from successful people is a necessity, not just in knowing yourself but also in empowering you to fulfill your greatest ability. Sometimes, it is not only about prayer, but also getting your eyes and ears open and finding out from successful people how they did it.

> Sometimes, it is not only about prayer, but getting your eyes and ears open and finding out from successful people how they did it.

Personally, this is one principle I adhere to a lot. In my life, I have identified some key successful personalities. I call them mentors. *A mentor is somebody who has made it and you desire to be like or even more than them.* Now the wisdom is to key into what they say, what made them reach high and far and then apply that to your life together with your own uniqueness.

This has helped me to discover my potentials even more and I have used that to walk in my divine calling. This does not however connote walking in people's shadows when you listen and learn from their mistakes, short comings and successes.

> There are two important days in a person's life. The day you were born and the day you discover why.

No, the truth is in what Solomon said, people have already made things happen and there is no point starting from the scratch when you can avoid some of their pitfalls and failures and even do better in the time frame you have.

It is just like a car that has just been made. If next year a new model should be made, the technicians will not completely avoid the old model but will take it into consideration, access it and out of that bring an improved version of the old. This is why every technological advancement on the market is always an improvement of the old. We all can learn from this.

It is not an accident that God gave us one mouth and two ears. That simply means God expects us to listen and learn more rather than doing the opposite. Honestly, some people really talk more than they listen. The more words you speak, the less they mean. So why overdo it?

The more you listen and learn more, the more you gain understanding. Somebody once said, open your ears wide and your eyes will understand. Again, when you listen and learn more, you turn to think right and are able to formulate and create new ideas.

John Maxwell once said, *"When we fail to listen, we shut out more than half of our learning potentials"*. That is why now, I don't just listen or even just read books, I write and summarise as much as I can and apply them to my life.

Now a question still arises. For instance when I go close to a successful person, what should I look out for? This is because people are more pruned to learn the short comings of most successful individuals than do their strengths. I give you 10 simple things you can learn from people you respect.

I. **Faithfulness**: Their level of commitment to God and to what they do.

II. **Integrity**: Is what they say in public what they do in private? Wholeness.

III. **Humility**: God resists the proud but makes room for the humble. Humility precedes honour.

IV. **Holiness**: Purity equals power. They must be Holy Spirit-addicted

V. **Relationship**: They must love and appreciate people and have their interest at heart.

VI. **Excellence**: They must be people of excellence. It is a good habit.

VII. **Passion**: Check their energy level. They must have passion for the right things.

VIII. **Priorities**: They must put first things first and always have the end in sight

IX. **Good family values**: They must be people who cherish and value family to the extent that, irrespective of many commitments, family remains first on their priority.

X. **Peace**: Those who seek peace with all men.

4. Identify both your natural and spiritual gifts:

There are two main kinds of gifts. These are your natural gifts and spiritual gifts.

Natural gifts are the talents you have been blessed with from birth. We are all born with natural talents. They are the gifts that can be seen physically. For instance, one's ability to play football, learn an instrument, gain a degree, establish a business easily all constitute natural or physical gifts.

Spiritual gifts are also gifts given by God's Holy Spirit spiritually. They are mostly referred to as gifts of the Spirit. Unlike natural gifts, these gifts manifest spiritually before being evident in the natural. Again, unlike natural gifts, you discover your spiritual gifts as you personally choose to walk with God on a personal level.

There are about nine different kinds of spiritual gifts beyond whatever natural gifts you have been blessed with. These are *Word of Wisdom, Word of Knowledge, Gift of Faith, Gifts of Healing, Working of Miracles, Gift of Prophecy, Discerning of Spirits, different kinds of Tongues, Interpretation of (different) Tongues*. Read 1 Corinthians 12, Isaiah 11:2-3, to understand more.

There is no doubt that majority of us are only aware of our physical gifts and not of our spiritual gifts. For us to achieve maximum productivity however requires us to also be aware of our spiritual gifts by walking closely with God on this journey to dominion. What this book is offering is to open you up to both your natural and spiritual gifts as you read.

There are two important days in a person's life. The day you were born and the day you discover why. To discover why and become fruitful with it involves knowing yourself and growing yourself. This is the power of self-awareness. You have the ability to be fruitful only when you know who you are and stop looking down on yourself but rather start walking in your kingdom dominion because you are a king.

APPLYING THE POWER OF SELF-DISCOVERY TO YOUR LIFE.
QUADRANT I (FRUITFULNESS) PRINCIPLE.

1. Your greatest enemy is ignorance of your God-given dominion. If you do not see value in yourself, you cannot add value to yourself. Begin therefore to identify your **strength, weakness, interest and opportunities.**

2. The key to pushing back the boundaries of your limitation is unlocking your seed of kingdom dominion.

3. Discover the power of self-discovery and begin the process of establishing your dominion by answering to yourself this set of questions:
   - **What do you have in your hands?**
   - **Who needs what you have?**
   - **What can you do with what you have?**

4. Consider the 5 factors of fear in this chapter. Which applies to your situation or conditions and how can you move your address to Faith Street?
   - **Fear of failure**
   - **Fear of trading security for the unknown**
   - **Fear of being overextended financially**
   - **Fear of what others will say or think**
   - **Fear that success will alienate peers.**

5. Taking personal responsibility for your actions, avoiding the blame game, making maximum use of your gifts and talents are what will make you yield productivity in life.
   - **Believe that you are Response –Able.**
   - **Believe in your abilities and be courageous to respond to them.**

❖ **Never forget the necessity of the 'Super' over your 'Natural' to achieve the extraordinary.**

6. Everybody needs a mentor. Do you have a mentor? Does he or she possess the 10 qualities listed in this chapter? Consider them carefully.

   I. **Faithfulness**: Their level of commitment to God and to what they do.

   II. **Integrity**: Is what they say in public what they do in private? Wholeness.

   III. **Humility**: God resists the proud but makes room for the humble. Humility precedes honour.

   IV. **Holiness**: Purity equals power. They must be Holy Spirit-addicted.

   V. **Relationship**: They must love and appreciate people and have their interest at heart.

   VI. **Excellence**: They must be people of excellence. It is a good habit.

   VII. **Passion**: Check their energy level. They must have passion for the right things.

   VIII. **Priorities**: They must put first things first and always have the end in sight.

   IX. **Good family values**: They must be people who cherish and value family to the extent that, irrespective of many commitments, family remains first on their priority.

   X. **Peace**: Those who seek peace with all men.

QUADRANT I

THE POWER OF IMAGINATION

Imagination determines everything

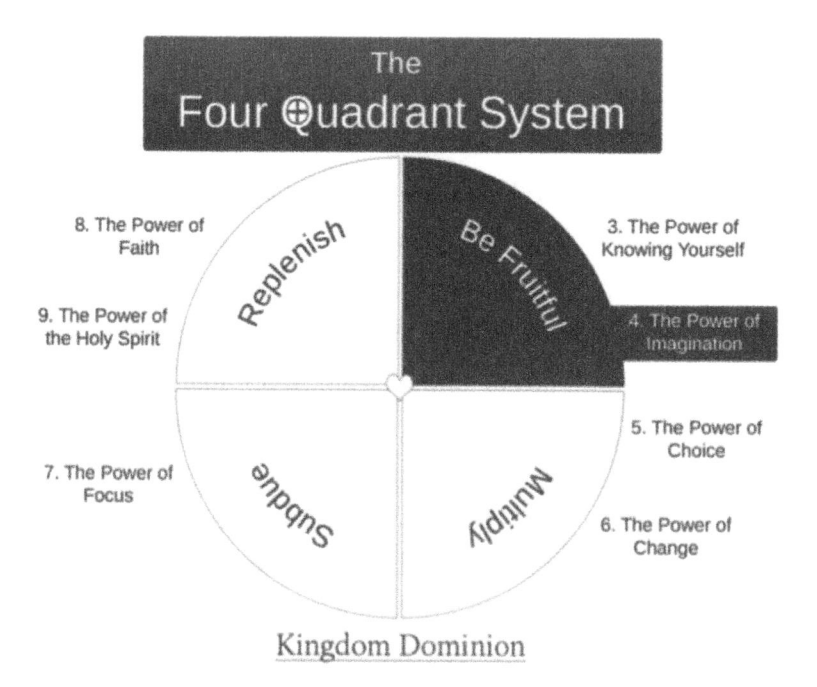

The Four Quadrant System

- Replenish
- Be Fruitful
- Multiply
- Subdue

8. The Power of Faith
9. The Power of the Holy Spirit
3. The Power of Knowing Yourself
4. The Power of Imagination
5. The Power of Choice
6. The Power of Change
7. The Power of Focus

Kingdom Dominion

4

THE POWER OF IMAGINATION

Fruitfulness begins in your imagination, which is one of the powerful abilities the Lord has bestowed on every human being. If you are to live at your fullest potential and be productive, one of the most important discoveries you have to make is unveiling the power of your thoughts.

Everything begins from the way you see and think through things. Our thoughts determine our actions which over time form our habits, character, destiny and reputations. Though this may go through a process, yet it all begins with our imagination.

> Everything begins from the way you see and think through things.

Imagination comes from the word 'imagine,' which simply means *your ability to visualize from far. Your ability to imagine comes from the part of your mind that thinks in pictures*. If we can see new ways and possibilities in our lives, we will actually discover that, there are actually no limits to what you have been created to achieve.

If you can just see it happen even when current situations prove otherwise, you can seize and realize it. You pose the ability to create in your mind beyond your current realities. Everything begins in your imagination. Before God created this world, the scripture in **Genesis 1** says the earth was void and without shape. God through His imagination shaped this world and brought it into existence.

- ❖ **How did He do this?**
- ❖ **Did He just wake up one day and just decide to create this world?**

No. I believe He had harboured this idea in Him before creation occurred. God had already seen this before He said it and when the moment came, He seized it. If you are to understand the existing and fulfilling journey of one's ability to imagine, follow God from **Genesis 1**, because this is where it all started.

> *"27 so God created humans in his image. In the image of God he created them. He created them male and female."* **Gen 1:27** (GW)

This means that, at this stage of creation, God had created man in His image to take over all that He had created. If this was not so, why then is it said in **Genesis 2:7** that,

> *"4 this is the account of heaven and earth when they were created, at the time when the Lord God made earth and heaven. 5 Wild bushes and plants were not on the earth yet because the Lord God hadn't sent rain on the earth. Also, there was no one to farm the land. 6 Instead, underground water would come up from the earth and water the entire surface of the ground. 7 Then the Lord God formed the man from the dust*

of the earth and blew the breath of life into his nostrils. The man became a living being" Gen 2:4-7 (GW)?

The two main scriptures above depicting the works of God shape the foundation of the principle of the *law of two creations*, which simply states that *all things are created twice*. That is, there is first a mental and second a physical creation of things.

In **Genesis 1:27**, we learn how God created man in His image based on the principle of first creation, which is based on imagination, thought and ideas. Man (male and female) was at this point created in God's Spirit but, even though man was created at this level, he was just an idea in the spiritual realm. This is true even in Chapter 2:5, where we learn that the reasons why plants and grains had not grown on the earth were two:

First, there was no rain,
Second, there was no one (man) there to farm the land.

It was not until in **Chapter 2:7** that God actually formed man, which represents the second creation, which is the real manifestation of God's thought. What God had conceived became a reality at the end. What first was just a thing of God's imagination could now be touched, seen and communicated with.

To explain further, notice the word *created* in **chapter 1 verse 27** and *formed* in **chapter 2 verses 7**. The word *Create* is to make something out of nothing, meaning that though God created man, He first created man out of

> The extent of our Fruitfulness depends on our power of imagination.

nothing that can be seen, which was why man was not there initially to farm the land. This is the power of an imagination, *the ability to think in the midst of unseen evidence.* The word *form* on the other hand means to make something out of something and here, God physically made man out of the dust of the earth and blew the breath of life into his nostrils.

Today, you are partakers of this incredible nature of the Creator. This explains why the law of two creations can be seen in every successful activity of man. You cannot construct a house without first having your imaginations in the form of architectural design before the physical house is built. The cars, home cinemas, etc. are first a thing of somebody's imaginations or thoughts before fruition.

Before you embark on a journey, you plan first in your mind before the actual journey. Before you begin a business, you first sit down and plan the type of business, where, what to sell, the capital involved before the actual business materialises, etc.

This strengthens the truth that our ability to be fruitful (productive) according to God's Word must first come from our imaginations and thought patterns. Author Steven Covey puts it this way, *"we are either the second creation of our own proactive design or we are the second creation of other people's personal agendas, or circumstances or of past habits"*

Components of Your Imagination.

What constitutes your imagination? As we define how powerful your imagination can be, let's try to break it down into its core elements and understand its ingredients. When we talk of the power of your imagination, what is it made of? Understanding this will help you to fulfil quadrant one (fruitfulness) and even beyond.

> Idea outlives you. Man dies but an idea never dies.

1. IDEA

Everything that exists started as an idea. Jonathan Hill once said *"ideas are the beginning points of all fortunes"*. Genesis 1 clearly attests to this fact that we were all an idea in the creator's mind before He expressed us. There is nothing in the world more powerful than an idea. An idea simply comes from your mind and therefore your imagination.

The clothes you are wearing, the table you are sitting on, the television you are so glued to and indeed everything you see all started as an idea. In fact, ideas rule the world. The poor man is not the one who does not have money but one who does not have an idea. This is because when you have an idea, you can implement it and you will never be poor in life.

Your idea outlives you. In other words, if you can just write down an idea and die, even your next of kin can implement that idea to work. So man dies but an idea never dies. You cannot destroy an idea even if it is a bad one. The only thing you can do to a bad idea is to turn it around into a good one.

What therefore is an idea? An idea is *an expressed imagination*. It is *a thought existing in the mind which when expressed has the power and capacity to lead you to greatness*. We are all naturally endowed with this creativity and all you have to do is activate this authority and be in charge of your life, destiny and purpose. So God has not only mandated you to be fruitful, multiply, replenish and subdue, He has also equipped you with what you need to fulfil this command, one of which is your ability to imagine.

An idea consists of two words: **CONCEPT** and **PRECEPT.** Before an idea becomes an excellent thought, it goes through these two processes. Precept: comes from two main words, *Pre* and *Cept*.

The Power Of Imagination

Pre means *before an idea*. Cept means *thought*. So the word precept simply means *before a thought*. This is how powerful God has made you that even before you think, you are already powerful.

Concept: comes from the word *conceived*, which simply means a *conceived idea*. So your idea is a direct product of your power of imagination. Putting these two together, we learn that God has even made us powerful even before a thought and more powerful when we begin to exercise and conceive ideas.

> Jesus Christ is God's idea manifested on two legs.

In John **1:1(ASV)** the Bibles says *"In the beginning was the Word, and the Word was with God, and the Word was God"*. Precious one, this verse simply tells you that God's word is He. You cannot separate His word from Him. That is why His word means so much to Him. This also explains why He always wants us to take every word from Him serious. His word is also His original idea from His imagination to man.

So anytime God gives you a word, for instance, it is an idea. You cannot see it and it lacks any physical evidence, but the good thing is, God's word or idea to you never stays like that forever, but at the appropriate moment manifests into something you can see and touch. What do I mean? Come with me to **verse 14** of the same **John 1.** *"14 And the Word became flesh, and dwelt among us (and we beheld his glory, glory as of the only begotten from the Father), full of grace and truth."*

The word or idea of God became flesh in the person of our Lord and Master Jesus Christ. We can therefore say that when an idea manifests, two things happen according to the word above. First, **it dwells with you**. You can touch it and feel it. It ceases to be an imagination at this point. The word *Dwell* is a Hebrew word which means *to occupy (as a mansion) or to reside.*

Second, **we beheld his glory**. In your ideas and imaginations lie your greatest glories in life, so do not destroy what God has freely given you. Glory simply means light, which is simply the opposite of shame. It also means the weight of something great. If God's idea manifests, so can your ideas be fruitful too. So begin by writing your ideas down and be ready to dwell in them.

2. THOUGHT

Another very important component of your ability to imagine is the way you think. We all think but the question is *how do you think?* Your thought makes you. This is why the bible states it in **Proverbs 23:7a** that *"as a man thinks in his heart so is he"*. There is a war being waged in all of us and just like **Joyce Meyer** always says, *"the battlefield of this war is in our mind"* (where all thought comes from)

Over the years, there is a quote that has always challenged my life to be careful of the way I think as person and I believe it can challenge you too. It says

> **"If you sow a thought, you reap an act**
> **If you sow an act, you reap a habit**
> **If you sow a habit, you reap a character"**

To start with, your thought is a seed, and secondly, just like any seed in your hands, you sow it. Now we all know that when a seed is sown, it follows a process and, after a period, bears fruit of its kind. What we usually refer to as seed time harvest. This is the power of your thought.

The Power Of Imagination

To think is simply to *activate your mind*. To think is also a *precept or concept that has the power to manifest over a period of time*. When you wake up in the morning, the first thought that comes into your mind concerning your life, job, marriage, problems and conditions is considered as a seed you are sowing.

A simple thought in your mind has the capacity to grow to reproduce effects over your life, whether positive or negative. This level is very important because a man's thought has something to do with his soul. Your soul comprises your thoughts, feelings and emotions.

> Just because a thought comes in to your mind does not mean you have to think it. Rather fill your mind with the word of God.

According to the word of God, the spirit and the soul work together and that is why you cannot afford to think negative, no matter the circumstance, because it will begin to affect your power to fulfill quadrant one (fruitfulness). Stress, worry, doubt, all are as a result of negative thinking. The key is that you have the power and ability to choose your thoughts daily.

"*Thy word have I hid in mine heart, that I might not sin against thee.*" **Psalm 119:11 (KJV)**. The Hebrew meaning for the word <u>heart</u> also means <u>mind;</u> meaning you can make a deliberate attempt to hide God's truth in your mind.

Heart or mind here also refers to the inner man. That part of you that go beyond your consciousness into your subconsciousness. It is the software inside the hardware we can easily see. This is what even the psychologists refer to as the sub-conscious mind.

Instead of dwelling on negative thoughts, the Lord appeared to Joshua and advised him on how to be successful and prosperous in all his dealings. The key is to meditate on the word of God.

*"This book of the law shall not depart out of **thy mouth**; but thou shalt **meditate** therein day and night, that thou mayest **observe** to do according to all that is written therein: for then thou shalt make thy way prosperous, and then thou shalt have good success."*
Joshua 1:8 (KJV)

The keys to success and prosperity lie in this statement above and not only Joshua but you too can obey it and taste good success. The words in bold constitute the three keys to good success and prosperity. *Do not let this book of the law depart from your mouth* (**speak it**), *meditate on it day and night* (**think it**) and be careful to do whatsoever is written in it (**act it**).

Do not forget that the words we speak concerning our lives, family, business, etc. are seeds which grow to become fruits. The same can be said of our thoughts and the way we act or behave. They all determine productivity in our lives, *for then shall your way be made prosperous and successful.*

> Failure to act on your ideas, imagination and thoughts shuts up your system of productivity and fruitfulness.

Components of a Thought

I. When you have sown a thought, you reap an act.

In life, there are two things that happen when you begin to think or imagine. It is either you act or you are acted upon. For you to successfully fulfill quadrant I, you must act and not be acted upon. In order words, the decision to bear fruits in life is best when it comes from you.

To act therefore is to take initiatives, to be more resourceful in our thinking. It takes action or initiative to fulfill potential and become what you have been mandated to become. Though God has naturally created you to be fruitful, multiply, replenish and subdue, it takes action to see results and growth in our lives. Failure to act on your ideas, imagination and thoughts shuts up your system of productivity and fruitfulness.

II. When you sow an act, you reap a habit.

When you continue to think about the same things you think about daily, it becomes a habit. You will never become fruitful in life until you learn to change something you do daily. You may not know the future but you know the habits you have and it is those habits (positive or negative) that will decide your future.

Habits are powerful factors in our quest to fulfill our dominion mandate because they are constant and over time determine our character and produce our effectiveness. This is why God advises us to meditate, ponder, contemplate and practice His word until it becomes a habit.

Habit is something that you love and, as a result, you do always. The principle, 'love what you do and do what you love' is very true; however, you must be careful not to apply this principle negatively because it will affect you. At this level of thinking, what starts just as a thought begins to become a habit, a positive thought becomes a positive habit and a negative thought becomes a negative habit. Aristotle once said, *"We are what we repeatedly do, excellence therefore is not an act, but a habit"*.

Whether negative or positive, it begins to become part of you and affects your life, business,

> For an animal to bite you, it usually comes from your own clothes.
> **Ghanaian proverb**

leadership and even your marriage accordingly. Breaking bad habits such as selfishness, laziness, procrastination and pride takes a tremendous effort and affects basic principle of fulfilling the first quadrant of fruitfulness. On the other hand, we can use positive habits to create the motivation, discipline and consistency we need for effective living.

So the question is, what habits are you developing? Like **Michael Angier** said, *"if you develop the habits of success, you will make success a habit"*

III. When you sow a habit, it becomes a character.

The character of a man is always a product of his thoughts. This is why your thoughts are very important. It takes time to develop character, whether good or bad. It is first a thought, and then you act upon it for a while, until it becomes a habit before becoming a character.

Character is who a person is. It is the real you. It forms the foundation of success or failure in our lives. Your character affects your integrity, humility, courage and patience in life. We develop character when our habits grow deep within our nature. The beginning of all of these is from your imaginations or thoughts.

IV. Going beyond our limitations.

The ability to create in our minds beyond our current limitations also has a major part to play in becoming productive in life. A limitation is a boundary, a restricted or final point in life. There are different forms of limitations ranging from *social, physical or personal to spiritual and even legal limitations*. We must admit that while some limitations are for good purposes, most limitations are debauched or evil. For instance, there are:

a. Personal Limitations.

These are self-imposed limitations such as allowing fear or anxiety to limit you from achieving quadrant one (fruitfulness). Your health condition can limit your movements and even what to eat. As a writer, you are limited by words. Your body has limited capacity in terms of the amount of food it can take at a time.

b. People or Public Limitation.

This is limitation from people. For instance, when somebody tells you that this is how far you can go in life, such a person is drawing a limitation for you and this is bad. It can be your boss at work, church or the denomination you join.

I remember quite clearly when some prominent people in my life told me that my first book will not go far so I should not be so keen on it. I ignored it and today it is those key people who are congratulating me on its success.

Beloved, people you even love can talk you down. They can limit your ability to be fruitful and produce results. A **Ghanaian proverb** says *"For an animal to bite you, it usually comes from your own clothes"*. You must beware of this so you can overcome any public hurdle and fulfill your dominion mandate. .

c. Protective Limitation.

These are the good ones to protect you. The traffic light is set to protect you from getting knocked down by a vehicle. The sea has a boundary it is limited to by God. Water from the seas, oceans, etc., covers over two-thirds of this world and imagine it was boundless– we would all be dead by now. So this is a good limitation. **Psalm**

33:7 (NLT) *"He gave the sea its boundaries and locked the oceans in vast reservoirs."*

d. Principalities Limitation

These are spiritual limitations. As long as the spirit controls the physical, there is no doubt then that evil forces in the spiritual realm will try to limit you from reaching your potential.

The bible states clearly that *"For we wrestle not against flesh and blood, but against principalities, against powers, against the rulers of the darkness of this world, against spiritual wickedness in high places. 13Wherefore take unto you the whole armour of God, that ye may be able to withstand in the evil day, and having done all, to stand."* **Ephesians 6:12-13 (KJV)**

"No matter how many times a man is imprisoned, you cannot imprison his power of imagination"–**Mensah Otabil**. The Apostle Paul is one man who was put behind bars many times of his life. The purpose was to stop him from spreading the Gospel of Jesus Christ, but do you know that they could not really stop him?

They were able to restrict his movements but not his ability to think and write. Though incarcerated most of his ministry life, he was able to write a major part of the New Testament from these prisons.

In Philippians 4:4, while Paul was still in prison, he wrote to the Philippians and said, *"rejoice again, I say rejoice."* How can a man in prison write to those who are free to rejoice? He understood the gift God had given him. He still had the power to imagine that all will be well. He did not allow a prison limitation to stop him from imagining how possible things could become.

As human beings, we may be limited, but with our imaginations, we can push back the boundaries of our limitations. This unique ability of imagination allows us to create in our minds what we want our future to look like and empowers us to go ahead and make things happen.

In **1 Timothy 2:9**, He again wrote to Timothy, saying *"And because I preach this Good News, I am suffering and have been chained like a criminal. But the word of God cannot be chained.*

Paul understood the power of God's word in us. Nothing is more potent than a man who thrives and dwells on the word of God. The word has the power to affect your imagination and break you out of every yoke or burden you may be under right now and cause you to be fruitful.

> Greatness can never be caged; we can all flourish if we do not allow our external environment to destroy us.

❖

President Nelson Rolihlahla Mandela is a man who demonstrates to us how powerful our imagination can be. This great man in 1962 was arrested and convicted of sabotage and other charges, and sentenced to life in prison. Mandela served 27 years in prison, spending most of these years on Robben Island.

Following his release he became the President of South Africa. One would have imagined a man imprisoned for 27 years to have been destroyed in body, soul and spirit. They were successful in imprisoning his body, but failed to incarcerate his power of imagination. Though he was confined in all those years, he still managed to have thought outside the box or small prison they put him in.

President Mandela is a good example of a man who discovered the natural ability God has bestowed on all men and this is the main reason why we all call him great. He teaches us that greatness can never be caged and that we can all flourish if we do not allow our external environment to destroy us.

Similarly, **Victor Frankl**, a determinist raised in the tradition of Freudian psychology. *Frankl was a psychiatrist and a Jew. He was imprisoned in the death camp of Nazi Germany where he experienced things that were so repugnant to our sense of decency that we shudder to even repeat.*

His parents, brother and his wife died in the camps or were sent to the gas ovens. Frankl himself suffered torture and innumerable indignities, never knowing from one moment to the next whether his path will lead to the ovens or if he would be among the saved who will remove the bodies or shovel out the ashes of those fated.

One day, naked and alone in a small room, he began to become aware of what was latter called the last of human freedom". They could control his entire environment, they could do what they wanted to his body, but Frankl himself was self-aware. In the midst of his experiences, Frankl would project himself into different circumstances, such as lecturing to his students after his release from the death camps. He could decide within himself, how all these were going to affect him. (Stephen Covey, The 7 Habit of Highly Effective People, pg 69)

The point of this inexplicable story of Frankl is how he used the powers of his imagination to think outside the box. Though limited by his captors, they could only control the environment he was but not influence his thought pattern. Frankl teaches us that in the midst of deep obstacles one can discover his purpose. His ability to reflect and imagine in the midst of pain equips us to also go beyond our external environment and never allow it to destroy us.

In the same way, every human being has been endowed with this ability to project himself from even the worst possible scenario we can think of, such as in the case of Victor Franklin. The reason is that we are created in the nature of God and we are partakers of His exact nature.

What the mind needs to fulfil quadrant one (fruitfulness)

The most important question you need to ask yourself is what does your mind need? The mind operates as a whole continent of its own because it has the ability to create, make, destroy and control people and even a nation. In order to tap into and make full use of its endowed abilities, you need to constantly fill it up.

Dr Mike Murdock puts it this way, *"your mind is a garden and you the Gardener. You sow in it, water it, uproot unwanted weeds and reap what you sow"*. In other words, nobody takes care of your imagination but you.

1. Your mind needs the word of God

The first and most important thing your mind needs is the Word of God. This is all you will ever need in your life. You can never make a mistake by filling your imaginations with God's words. His word contains His exact nature, presence and power to overcome and succeed. You need to continuously chart with your mind. Practically, speak into your imaginations the word of God.

> Do not lose sight of the future. Once you have seen the future, decide to live there.

In **Ezekiel 3:1 (NLT)**, the Lord practically told His servant to eat the word. *"The voice said to me, "Son of man, eat what I am giving you—eat this scroll! Then go and give its message to the people of Israel."*

You can practically eat the word of God by studying it and filling your mind with it. The verse continues that, when you eat the word, it first ***becomes sweet to your lips*** and secondly ***bitter in your stomach***. The word is first sweet to your lips because God's words bring encouragement, peace, confidence, joy and positive strength to your life and imagination.

It becomes bitter to your stomach because what is bitter gets vomited out. When you have consciously and practically dwelt on God's Word, you will reap its result.

"Finally, brethren, whatsoever things are true, whatsoever things are honest, whatsoever things are just, whatsoever things are pure, whatsoever things are lovely, whatsoever things are of good report; if there be any virtue, and if there be any praise, think on these things." **Philippians. 4:8 (KJV)**

2. Your mind needs a Vision

Visions are clear mental pictures of a better tomorrow given by God. Many people lack a vision for their lives, family, work, community and even country. However, vision is key, without it an individual or even a nation perishes. What we need is to conceive vision for our lives through the power of our imaginations because as Mary Wollstonecraft Shelley pointed out more than a hundred years ago: "Nothing contributes so much to tranquilize the mind as a steady purpose-a point on which the soul may fix its intellectual eye."

A Biblical example is the young man Joseph. Joseph had a vision of the future 0at an early stage in his life. He saw what the Lord could do with his life (Genesis 37:5). He remained determined to act and not be acted upon. This is the **SEE it** level.

The Power Of Imagination

SAY it. When you see a vision, move forward to saying it. Only be wise to have prayed about your vision more so that people will not begin to envy you. Joseph not only saw a vision, he also said it though his brothers hated him the more.*"Listen to this dream," he announced. 7"We were out in the field tying up bundles of grain. My bundle stood up, and then your bundles all gathered around and bowed low before it!"* **Genesis 37:6-7 (NLT).**

One major key to seeing and saying your vision is that it helps you to keep public commitment, thus once you say it, you will be more responsible, thus making sure you do not disappoint. This will also help you to know who loves or hates you. After you have said what you see,

SOW into it: pray about the vision constantly, work hard towards it, spend time and plan. These are all seeds you must sow to keep the dream alive. Joseph had to be sold to Potiphar's house, tested by his wife and thrown into prison, before realising the vision.

> If you can manage your imaginations, you can manage your life.

These are all seeds he sowed towards harvesting the vision. Joseph also sowed the seed of prayer, that's why the presence of God was with him throughout his journey to the level that Potiphar even noticed it (Genesis 39:2-3). Joseph's faith was deep, so should yours. When you have sowed into the vision

SEIZE it: God creates seasons, man makes time; He avails, and man must prevail. When there comes a grand opening to manifest in your vision, do not waste precious time and opportunities; always seize your Kairos moment.

3. The mind needs a focus:

Your mind will never succeed without a clear objective or a goal. When you see the vision, focus on it. Do not lose sight of the future. Once you have seen the future, decide to live there. Quit attempting everything.

The only way you can do that in this weary world is to focus your energy on that vision, looking neither to the left nor to the right. *"No, dear brothers and sisters, I am still not all I should be, but I am focusing all my energies on this one thing: Forgetting the past and looking forward to what lies ahead, 14I strain to reach the end of the race and receive the prize for which God, through Christ Jesus, is calling us up to heaven.* **Philippians 3:13-14 (NLT).**

Apostle Paul focused all his energy on one thing. After Joseph had seen the vision, he focused solely on it. Why do you think they both did this? Focus will give you enough energy to tap into your well of strength and expand you to actualise the vision.

Thinking Skills of Quadrant one (fruitful) people.

Finally, to end this chapter, let's discover what will make you a quadrant one person in your walk into dominion. The difference between those who make it and those who do not mostly is in the way of imagination or thought.

In his book, *How successful people think*, author **John Maxwell** outlines 11 key ways of thinking of successful people and I believe that they are qualities of a quadrant one person.

- ❖ **Big Picture Thinking**: Your ability to think beyond yourself and your world.
- ❖ **Focused Thinking**: The ability to think with clarity by removing distraction and clusters.

- ❖ **Creative Thinking**: Ability to break out of yourself and explore new ideas.
- ❖ **Realistic Thinking**: Ability to build a solid foundation on facts and principles.
- ❖ **Strategic Thinking**: Your ability to implement plans that increase potential tomorrow.
- ❖ **Reflective Thinking**: Your ability to revisit the past and gain perspective for the future.
- ❖ **Questioning Popular Thinking**: Ability to reject common thinking and gain new ideas.
- ❖ **Possibility Thinking**: Ability to believe even in the impossible to solve problems.
- ❖ **Shared Thinking**: Ability to include others to go beyond our own thoughts.
- ❖ **Unselfish Thinking**: Ability to consider others and think with collaboration.
- ❖ **Bottom Line Thinking**: Ability to focus on results and reap the best out of every task.

APPLYING THE POWER OF IMAGINATION/ THOUGHT TO YOUR LIFE
QUADRANT I PRINCIPLE (FRUITFULNESS)

1. The extent of our fruitfulness is dependent on our imagination and thought process. What do you plan of doing or becoming?
2. When you fail to act on your ideas, imaginations and thoughts, you shut up your system of productivity and fruitfulness.
3. In what ways can you initiate a move that can propel changes in your life? What vision do you have for your life, work, ministry, organisation and nation?
4. What character or habit do you need to change to improve yourself, business, ministry or even family to develop the motivation, discipline and consistency to be fruitful?
5. Identify what are your areas of limitation and deal with them. Be it:
   - **Personal**
   - **People or public**
   - **Principalities (evil).**
6. Remember that though you may be limited, you can push back the boundaries of your limitation with your imagination by setting your mind on positive things.
7. Both Nelson Mandela and Victor Frankl are good examples of how powerful our imagination can be. Nelson Mandela teaches us that greatness can never be caged and that we can all flourish if we do not allow our external environment to destroy us

   Frankl teaches us that in the midst of deep obstacles one can discover his purpose. His ability to reflect and imagine in the

midst of pain equips us to also go beyond our external environment and never allow it to destroy us.
8. Figure out what your mind needs to create and think? Let the suggestions in this chapter help you.
   - ❖ **Your mind needs the Word of God: consciously and practically dwell on God's Word.**
   - ❖ **Your mind need a vision: A vision is a mental picture of a better tomorrow.**
   - ❖ **Your mind needs to focus on correct principles.**
9. Develop good thinking skills by following the 11 principles shared in this book from John Maxwell's book, "How successful people think.".

QUADRANT 2 (MULTIPLY)

THE POWER OF CHOICE

Choices determine destinies

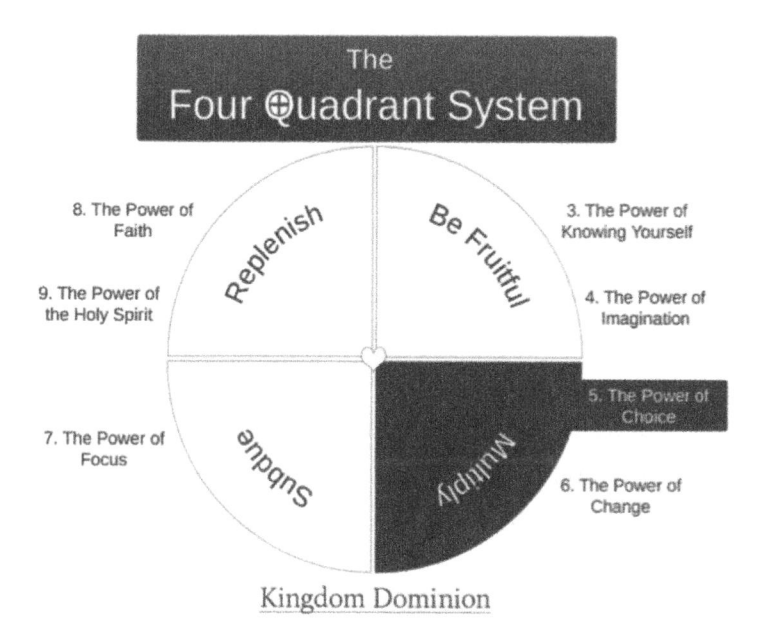

The Four Quadrant System

- 8. The Power of Faith
- 9. The Power of the Holy Spirit
- 7. The Power of Focus
- 3. The Power of Knowing Yourself
- 4. The Power of Imagination
- 5. The Power of Choice
- 6. The Power of Change

Replenish · Be Fruitful · Subdue · Multiply

Kingdom Dominion

5

THE POWER OF CHOICE

One major key to multiplying your fruitfulness on your call to rule is through the choices that you will make. You will agree with me that making choices in life is one of the most important, yet sensitive areas to even talk or write about. Of all the human abilities God granted us, perhaps making our own choices remains a determining factor in how our lives turn out. Making wrong choices in life will result in negative outcomes, whereas making right decisions in life will make us sail through it more easily.

> Our greatest power in life is our ability to choose.

Right choices in life position us to live in the abundance of life, which is a direct activity of divine inspiration by which, through the foundation of God's principles, your dominion mandate can go further to multiplying your fruits. The choices we make, especially the good ones, help us to seize opportunities so that our future will not be worse.

No wonder some people argue that our greatest power in life is our ability to choose. The divine mandate to be fruitful, multiply, replenish and subdue has been given to mankind, but it takes

The Power Of Choice

a personal and corporate decision to realise this. To understand this point, we must go back to creation, where it all started. When God created man, He gave man two very important things. The first was *His presence a*nd the second *choice*.

God originally created man for relationship and fellowship. Every day He will come down to the Garden of Eden to talk and fellowship with man until one day, man chose to do the things God warned him not to.

> *"And the Lord God took the man, and put him into the garden of Eden to dress it and to keep it. 16And the Lord God commanded the man, saying, Of every tree of the garden thou mayest freely eat: 17But of the tree of the knowledge of good and evil, thou shalt not eat of it: for in the day that thou eatest thereof thou shalt surely die."* **Genesis 2:15-17 (KJV)**

As you can see above, God gave man everything, with the exception of one thing: He did not physically prevent him from eating. Rather than totally preventing man from eating or even avoiding it from the garden completely, God gave man a choice and man made the wrong choice. God still gives man choices and most of the time we still make the wrong choices.

You may ask why did God give man His presence and still offer him freedom to choose? Without choices, there cannot be judgement. We would all be prisoners. The purpose of this important ability to choose is to offer God the opportunity to judge mankind. This is why our greatest test in life lies between choosing to obey God or to be disobedient to Him.

"I call heaven and earth to record this day against you, that I have set before you life and death, blessing and cursing: therefore choose life, that both thou and thy seed may live."
Deuteronomy. 30:19 (KJV)

Our choices demonstrate to God and ourselves, who we truly are, more than any other abilities we have.

And if it seem evil unto you to serve the Lord, choose you this day whom ye will serve; whether the gods which your fathers served that were on the other side of the flood, or the gods of the Amorites, in whose land ye dwell: but as for me and my house, we will serve the Lord.
Joshua 24:15 (KJV)

What am I trying to tell you? Our choices demonstrate to God and ourselves, who we truly are, more than any other abilities we have.

C.S Lewis *observed, every time you make a decision, you are turning the central part of you, the part that chooses* <u>in to</u> *something a little different from what it was before. Taking your life as a whole, with all your innumerable choices, you are slowly turning this central thing into a heavenly creature or* <u>a</u> *into a hellish creature"*

What is important for us to note is that, in the midst of our free will, we recognise the importance of the hand of God, His voice and His power to abide in our choices and decisions daily so we can be assured of not just becoming, fruitful, but also moving forward towards multiplying them and even beyond.

Truth about choices

1. Every choice we make in life has consequences. Just as choosing to obey God and His principles attracts His blessings to your life, disobeying Him attracts curses too. In our daily choices in life, it is the same. The choices we make daily make us. It is what moves us to multiply what we already have.

2. Sometimes the choices we make in life can affect not only us but our entire generation.

The sins of Adam and Eve affected the whole of mankind until Christ came to redeem us. Consider someone like Achan in the Bible; his sin affected not only him but his entire generation, including even his animals.

> *"And Joshua, and all Israel with him, took Achan the son of Zerah, and the silver, and the garment, and the wedge of gold, and his sons, and his daughters, and his oxen, and his asses, and his sheep, and his tent, and all that he had: and they brought them unto the valley of Achor."* **Joshua 7:24 (KJV)**

That is why you have to be careful what you are doing now, because it may be your children and grandchildren who may suffer for it or be blessed by it, after you are gone.

> The power to choose right in the midst of bad condition and circumstance has been given to you by God to help in all you will do in life.

3. My choices today will determine my future tomorrow. This is just like the sowing and reaping principle. You cannot choose to live recklessly today and expect all to be well with you tomorrow.

Disobedience will only beget disobedience, which will be a curse over your own future.

Eleanor Roosevelt puts it this *way "One's philosophy is not best expressed in words; it is expressed in the choices one makes. In the long run, we shape our lives and we shape ourselves."*

4. **Not all choices carry equal value:** It is said that the average home today in Europe has more than 20 channels of Television to choose from. Certainly, trying to choose one to watch cannot be compared to facing a life-threatening decision in life.

Some people even struggle about what to choose to eat because too many choices make decisions tough, but when you are faced with some tough choices in life such as what career path you should take, woman or man you should marry ... such choices carry heavy weight.

5. **To make right choices from the wrong, forget the past and focus on the present.** We all make mistakes. Sometimes I wish I could go back to yesterday and change some decisions I have made, but I cannot. The same applies to you. You have got to let go of the past to make the right choices today. It does not matter what you have done in the past, God's grace is sufficient -for you today. Like Paul said, *one thing I do, forgetting the past* (Philippians 3:13). Understand that your yesterday ended last night.

However, if you have some past victories, you can look back to the past to empower you to make more right choices in the present. For David to have defeated Goliath one of the things he did was to recount his victories from past experiences and that helped to choose and then win over the giant.

"David said moreover, The Lord that delivered me out of the paw of the lion, and out of the paw of the bear, he will deliver

me out of the hand of this Philistine. And Saul said unto David, Go, and the Lord be with thee." **1 Samuel 17:37 (KJV)**

So in past losses, learn to let go and make a right decision today. On the other hand, let past victories inspire you for more good choices.

6. **For every step in life, there is a decision to make.** This simply tells you that you cannot run away from ever making choices in life. Remember it is the second most important power God has given you aside His exact presence, which is the Holy Spirit, the super natural Person Who gives supernatural ability as you will read about later in this book. There is a choice you always will make in life if you want to keep growing, increasing and fulfilling your mandate.

7. **It is not what happens to us, but our response to what happens to us, that matters.** Things will always happen to us as long as for every step in life there is a decision to make. We have the power to choose our response daily. You may not be able to stop somebody from hurting your feelings but you can choose not to allow what he or she says to affect you.

> Earth (our ability) has no sorrow heaven (His presence) cannot solve. There is no situation He cannot fix in your life.

This is the power of choice. It is the ability to choose your response in the midst of misery, deception, bitterness and more. Happiness is a choice you make. When you wake up in the morning feeling sad or depressed, you can quickly change your thinking back to feeling good and full of faith. The powers to choose right in the midst of bad condition and circumstance have been given to you by God to help you in all you will do in life.

How to make the right choices in life?

This is one very important question we all sometimes ask. How do I make the right choices or decisions in life? It is no doubt that making life-changing choices sometimes can be difficult. Because of this, most people refuse to even take decisions they ought to make. The sad thing is that, it is either you learn to choose or others will make your choices for you and you may not like the outcome.

Just because making decisions are tough does not mean that you should leave your decisions to chance. The ability to choose right resides in you and just like the rest of the abilities you are reading about in this book, you must activate it and use it for your benefit. To make the right decisions in life:

1. Identify the issue and locate a promise in the word of God.

I strongly believe that the first point to making a right choice in life is to identify what the issue is. It may mean writing it on a piece of paper. The problem or issue is? State it clearly, because for every problem, there is a possible solution, whether big or small.

The reason why you then locate a promise in the Word of God is that, it is not a mistake or coincidence that God gave us His presence and the ability to choose at the same time. He was simply expressing to us that, our ability to choose right will never function properly without His consented presence. He created us to choose, yes, but not without Him. That is why when He created man, He gave us both at the same time. Bear in mind that I am talking about life-changing choices here, for not all choices carry equal weight.

"Commit thy works unto the Lord, and thy thoughts shall be established". **Proverbs 16:3 (KJV)**

Earth (our ability) has no sorrow heaven (His presence) cannot solve. There is no situation He cannot fix in your life. Just like Solomon said, there is nothing new under the sun. As you locate a promise in the Word of God, usually you will find out that you are not alone, people have been before where you are now and their testimony can give you confidence to be strong.

After you have identified what the problem is, prayer is what you need to engage yourself in. Spend more time in prayer if you want to make the right choices in life, especially on your quest for fruitfulness. Praying God's word frequently is a seed you sow once you have identified your issue. Do you know that God's Word is a seed? It is all you need.

"The sower soweth the word". **Mark 4:14 (KJV)**

"Thy *word is a lamp unto my feet, and a light unto my path"*.
Psalm 119:105 (KJV)

The word is a seed, a lamp and light in grey areas of your life. Like a seed, sow it and God will cause it to grow. Prayer positions you to know what the right choices are once you are ready to make one.

2. Gather information and seek advice / counsel

As you identify the issue at hand, gather information about the choice you want to make. Today you can gather information through internet search engines, books, articles and even talking to the right people. The Bible even encourages us to seek counselling, for in the multitude of it lies wisdom.

"Without counsel purposes are disappointed: but in the multitude of counsellors they are established". **Proverbs 15:22 (KJV)**

"People who despise advice will find themselves in trouble; those who respect it will succeed. 14The advice of the wise is like a life-giving fountain; those who accept it avoid the snares of death." **Proverbs 13:13-14 (NLT)**

In seeking advice, it is important you know whose advice you are listening to because seeking the wrong information will be equal to the wrong choices being taken. In seeking advice, consider people who have had success in the area of your decision taking and also key stakeholders who must say yes before making the decision, such as spouses, parents and family. People who have your genuine interest at heart may also be considered. A good friend is worth listening to.

You may also consider people with good character and practical wisdom, meaning someone who has practical experience in the area you seek to grow or improve. Such people must also have the ability to keep secret, because you would not like your issue to be all over the place after talking to such a person.

An Italian proverb says, *"Keep Company with good men and you will increase their number."* *"A person's words can be life-giving water; words of true wisdom are as refreshing as a bubbling brook"*. **Proverbs 18:4 (NLT)**

On the contrary, in seeking advice, be careful of those who will put emotions and feelings before the reality you are facing. We live in an age where there are many voices of counsel, but few voices of vision; emotionally-loaded advice may not be what you need when making choices that will move you higher to your next level.

> *"Only the wise can give good advice; fools cannot do so."* **Proverbs 15:7 (NLT).** *I quite remember when I lost my father in a painful circumstance and did not know what to do, especially as I was out of my native country. I was faced with a life-changing decision: whether to stay where I was or return to bury him.*

3. Believe in the choices you make and give it a chance.

A lot of people, still after making a decision in life do not have the courage to execute that decision. Sometimes it is as a result of fear of failure, doubt, setback or someone deterring you from your goals. Doubt is the enemy to your manifestation. Your faith will never go beyond the question mark. We are simply what we believe.

You have got to give your choice a chance. The fact that it may be a life-changing decision does not mean you will not face challenges. To walk in dominion and move from fruit bearing to multiplication, make up your mind to fight defeat and discouragement and even if you fail, know that failure is never final. Try again until you win and when you have the confidence to give your choice a chance, you will come out with victory.

> Doubt is the enemy to your manifestation.

4. In giving your choice a chance, also learn to **walk in love and patience**. Your faith will not work without love and patience. Love is the single most important component in everything you do. You must be willing to love yourself and the decision in order to realise any possible positive outcome. Faith works by love, meaning your faith will never work if you do not love what your decision may be.

Patience is also a virtue in giving your choice a chance. You must not expect things to suddenly turn around if you are making a life-changing decision. Sometimes your decision may take a while before you see results. Being patient here is not putting up with negative issues but remaining consistent about the decision you have taken.

> *"My brethren, count it all joy when ye fall into divers temptations; 3Knowing this, that the trying of your faith worketh patience. 4But let patience have her perfect work, that ye may be perfect and entire, wanting nothing.* **James 1:2-4 (KJV)**

Patience is the price you pay for the things you want to get from life.

5. Make decisions on the principles and values you believe in.

In seeking to convert what you have to the next level (multiply), do not base all your hopes on people. Yes, it is true that you may have to consider the advice and counsel of wise and key people you believe in and trust. However, after seeking for people's opinion, you have got to separate yourself and make a choice out of the principles and values you believe in.

Remember, you have got to make that choice and not the people. Growth and fruitfulness will not come without separation. That is why Jesus always separated himself

> Facts always face the condition, whereas truth faces the expectation. Never let your conditions decide your expectation.

from the crowd anytime a major decision had to be made. *"Settle yourself in solitude and you will come upon Him in yourself"* **Teresa of Avila**. It is not about being lonely, I must warn. Loneliness is inner emptiness. Solitude is inner fulfillment.

The key to always making a good decision is to always learn to be you. In the midst of making key choices in life, always know that nobody feels the way you feel, though people may make you think otherwise. This is why your decision should rise from the principle and values you possess and cherish.

This may sound risky to do but remember there is no adventure without risk. Principles and values simply represent what you stand for as a person. The risky part here is that, what you stand for as a person may not necessarily be the majority's opinion, yet trust in your abilities to succeed.

Concerning my father's death, I remember making a decision to stay back after considering all that people had said. At the end, it boiled down to my principles and values. Though it was a difficult one, my principles were to give a befitting burial to my dad and still be in a position to help my younger siblings to further their education, rather than spend a handsome amount of money to travel back home and after everything, those same people will abandon me and leave me to my fate.

This was a big challenge for me, and so will it be for you when you are making a life-changing decision that can catapult you to greater results. There is no meaning in life without a challenge. In every difficult decision ahead of you lies a sense of purpose to your life. God will always test your character and integrity by the choices you make and this is where your values and principles matter.

The issue at hand may be great and difficult, but always remember that great testimonies and breakthroughs never happen without great issues.

6. In making choices, always learn to face inward reality:

Many a times, when people are in the process of making life-changing decisions, they tend to face the facts rather than the truth. Inward reality involves making decisions based on the truth rather than the facts. There is always a thin line between facts and truths. This truth is Jesus Christ who is the way to making great decisions.

> Loneliness is inner emptiness.
> Solitude is inner fulfillment.

Facts are usually the outward realities you may be facing, whereas truths are mostly based on what is inside of you. The fact of the matter usually puts you in bondage of fear and anxiety simply because the decision before you may be a difficult one. Facts always face the condition whereas truth faces the expectation. Never let your conditions decide your expectation.

Admittedly, you will always be faced by the facts or the impending situation, but when you are willing to know and live by the truth that is when freedom of making a right decision will be found. Jesus made it categorically clear when He said; *"you shall know the truth and the truth shall set you free."* **John 8:32**

Fear, worry, anxiety, ecstatic experiences or even good feelings will not give you freedom, only knowledge of the truth, and this is what inward reality concentrates on before the outward expression.

The truth will always stand out when we exercise and maximise our abilities rightly and carefully. We face inward reality when we ask timely questions and stay truthful to ourselves. The set of questions below can help you to narrow your choices and help you to negotiate rightly in every major decision you face in life.

- Am I called to do this?
- Am I going to grow and is this going to help my development?
- Is this the best option?
- Is this my heart beat?

Truthfully addressing some of these critical questions will help you to move your gifts, talents, and even channel your pains, in the right directions.

Choosing your chosen Destiny

As you read the power and ability to choose, it is important to understand that the ability to move from fruit bearing to fruit multiplication has little to do with our circumstance but is rather determined by our choices and the changes we are willing to make.

It is your sole responsibility to choose to move through the quadrants which I believe form part of God's chosen destiny for your life. The truth is, before you were born, God had already established your destiny. If you were a book in the hands of God, He had already finished reading you before your began life.

> *"I know, LORD, that a person's life is not his own. No one is able to plan his own course."* ***Jeremiah 10:23 (NLT)***

> *"You watched me as I was being formed in utter seclusion, as I was woven together in the dark of the womb. 16You saw me before I was born. Every day of my life was recorded in your book. Every moment was laid out before a single day had passed".*** Psalm 139:15-16 (NLT)***

Both verses above explain to you some key things about your chosen destiny:
1. **Your life is not your own**: God owns your life.
2. **Your course/ destiny has been planned by God**: He watched you being formed in your mother's womb even before you were born
3. **Your destiny or course is finished, you have been born to start** and the fact that you are alive is a sign that you have something to fulfill.

God is already committed to your destiny; the question is, are you ready to choose God's already chosen destiny for your life? This is the power of choice, the ability to make personal decisions whether you will live God's plan for your life or your plan for yourself.

Choosing to multiply your fruits

What choices do you have to make so that you can position yourself to move from quadrant one to two? How do you open up many opportunities or options for what you already have or even convert your gifts, talents, ideas or even your pains and failures into much better gains? After recognising your dominant gifts (fruits), how do you raise them to the highest level of excellence (multiply)?

To answer any of these questions above:

I. Open yourself to new revelations

The more you choose to open up yourself to be taught, the more you will discover greater ways to multiply what you have. More understanding is given to the man who shows the desire to learn new ways and methods of doing things.

You will agree with me that it is possible to have fruits without multiplying them, but there cannot be fruit multiplication without first having fruits to show forth. This is what makes the right choices and changes necessary for quadrant two (multiply). We can also make the right choices as we continuously open ourselves up to new revelations.

II. Discern the future ahead

Yielding higher increase always involves looking ahead into the future. No one moves higher by holding on to the past. Choosing to discern a greater future even in the midst of difficult challenges can help transform your gifts, talents, business and ministry to the next level.

III. Trust your intuition

Your intuition is usually what you know for sure but not for certain. For instance, have you ever been in a situation where you are convinced about a direction to take and yet having doubt about the outcome? In such cases, after praying about it, you have to trust your intuition (God given ability) and move forward.

> The greatest decision you will ever make is to choose to live the will of God concerning your life.

If you can follow most of the guidelines this book is suggesting, you can sense success a mile away to promote your growth into multiplying your efforts. You can also choose to go with your intuition by asking the right questions tailored to your situation and this will encourage you to understand your next level.

As long as your intuition is based on the godly principles offered in this book and beyond, I am sure all will be well with you; because though you may not know what the future holds, you can trust the One who knows the future to bring you to an expected end.

IV. Seek to work with others.

The attitude to bearing fruit should be based on the question, *what can I do for others?* However, to move from fruit bearing to increasing your capacity, gift, talents or whatever, you must change your attitude to *what can I do with others?*

It is always at the point of choosing to work with others for the greater good of mankind that quadrant two (multiply) and even the rest of the quadrants begin to unfold. The answer to multiplication is even written biblically as *"one will chase a thousand but two ten thousand."*

As we end this chapter, I trust you have learned something new. The power to choose has been given to you by God. Maximise it and use it wisely. The greatest decision you will ever make is to choose to live the will of God concerning your life. Once you have positioned your choices right, there is no way you will never move forward to bear fruit and multiply.

APPLYING THE POWER OF CHOICE QUADRANT 2 (MULTIPLY)

This chapter begins ideas and lessons in achieving quadrant two (multiplication). To multiply your fruits at this level, you need everything in quadrant one (imagination, self-discovery) together with what this chapter and the next suggest.

C.S Lewis observed, every time you make a decision, you are turning the central part of you, the part that chooses <u>in to</u> something a little different from what it was before. Taking your life as a whole, with all your innumerable choices, you are slowly turning this central thing into a heavenly creature or <u>a</u> into a hellish creature"

1. Apply these questions to your life.
   - ❖ **What are the consequences of your impending choices?**
   - ❖ **Who are the people your choices may affect today or in the immediate future? Study Achan's story in this Joshua 7.**
   - ❖ **Imagine what will be the outcome of your life, ministry, career, family based on your choices today?**
2. It is the desire of everyone to make the right choices that will lead to multiplication of gifts and abilities. To do this,
   - ❖ **Identify your area of necessity and gather as much information as possible.**
   - ❖ **Seek advice from wise people and those who have your best interest at heart**
   - ❖ **Learn to believe in your choices and give it a chance**
   - ❖ **Make your decisions based on correct principles and values you believe in. As a child of God, never forget the Holy Spirit.**
3. Critically evaluate yourself with:

- ❖ **Am I called to do this?**
- ❖ **Am I going to grow and is this going to help my development?**
- ❖ **Is this the best option?**
- ❖ **Is this my heart beat?**

4. To move from quadrant one to quadrant two with what you have:
   - ❖ **Open yourself, business, ministry to new revelations**
   - ❖ **Reflect and discern the future ahead**
   - ❖ **Work with the right people**

5. Finally always remember that the greatest decision to observe all the quadrants manifesting in your life is to choose to live your chosen destiny.

QUADRANT TWO

THE POWER OF CHANGE

Growth always equals change.

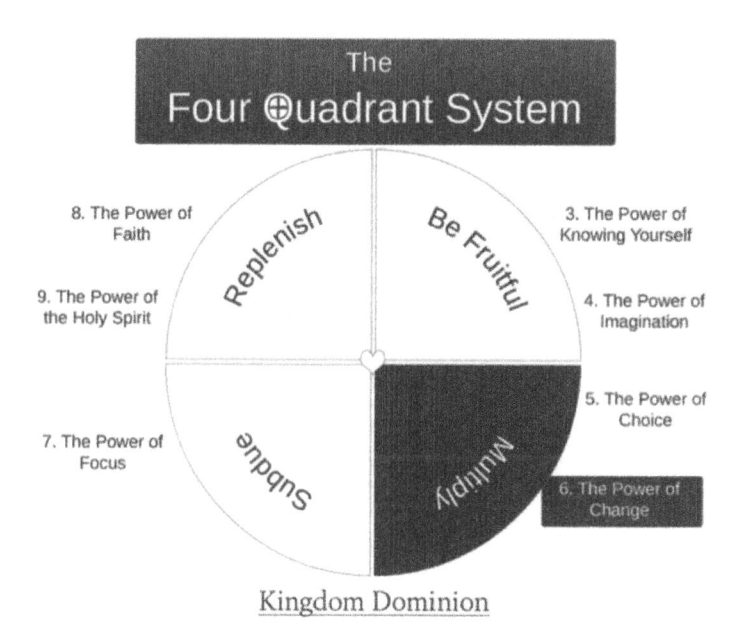

The Four Quadrant System

- 8. The Power of Faith
- 9. The Power of the Holy Spirit
- 7. The Power of Focus
- 3. The Power of Knowing Yourself
- 4. The Power of Imagination
- 5. The Power of Choice
- 6. The Power of Change

Replenish · Be Fruitful · Subdue · Multiply

Kingdom Dominion

6

THE POWER OF CHANGE

Change is one unique ability you have been endowed from the day you were born. You have the power to change your current situation if you do not like it. God created you with the ability to change things around you. The word 'change' simply means to transform or convert. It is to exchange for something better and befitting. Imagine buying a pair of shoes from a shop. You got home and it did not fit. What do you do? You take it back and change it.

> Change comes when we renew our thought patterns and the mind is renewed by applying it to those things that will transform it.

In this chapter, you will discover and understand how the power of change is also needed to **multiply** your fruits. Change comes when we renew our thought patterns and the mind is renewed by applying it to those things that will transform it. To change is to renew your mind by constantly freshening up and doing away with waste from life. It is mainly the changes and choices you make that lead you to discover many opportunities for multiplying your productivity in life.

The Power of Change

Do you know that the main reason behind Jesus' crucifixion was because He came to advocate change? The world did not understand His purpose for us. The first ever public statement that Jesus made was one to sensitise the world of a new order, the Kingdom of God.

"From that time Jesus began to preach, crying out, <u>Repent</u> (change your mind for the better, heartily amend your ways, with abhorrence of your past sins), for the kingdom of heaven is at hand." **Matthew 4:17 (AMP)**

Jesus was encouraging the world to receive God's Kingdom in which He was the King by changing our mind for the better. To change also includes amending our old ways of behaviour and attitudes. Your old ways of thinking must change if you are to take what you have to the next level of your dominion mandate. If you desire to multiply your fruits, change something you do daily. It can be your environment, thought process, prayer life, books you read and sometimes the friends you keep. There is an Italian proverb that says "*keep company with good men and you will soon increase their number.*" How true this is to all people.

Change is of essence in our time today. It is an ability you cannot do without because everything in this world changes. A movie I watched had the title *"The day the earth stood still"* and in that movie, the world stood still for a minute. Can you imagine what will happen when earth decides to stop rotating? Everything in this world will begin to fall.

There will be pandemonium on earth, chaos everywhere. We will all begin to die and this is what was depicted in the movie. This shows how necessary this ability is to you; especially if you want to

The Four Quadrants To Greatness.

move what you have (fruits) to the next level (multiply). If you want to grow from just bearing fruits to multiplying them and beyond, then you must be ready for change. Everything is moving forward so you cannot decide to stay as you are and expect to grow.

You may have probably heard of the phrase growth = change. For you to grow from one quadrant to the other involves the choices and changes you make. This is why these two principles are being taught after fruit production. The difference between the Dead Sea and a river is that the latter is constantly moving forward but the former is not. A river flows, constantly allowing new levels of water to regularly come in and out of its banks, while a sea is considered dead when it allows little or no level of water to flow in or out of its banks.

> Growth = change.

As a result, there is no life in the Dead Sea. It does not support any aquatic nature. In short, anything that tries to live in the Dead Sea dies because the sea refuses to accept change. This is the same in our lives. When man refuses to change for the better, it is only a matter of time before we expire (and we would have contributed to our own demise).

We live in a world of technological advancement. There are constant changes on the market. You think you have bought the latest television, car, fridge, house and more, only to find out the next day that there are new models in town. These are all the impact of change. The funny thing is that, in the midst of all these, a new model, for instance of a car, is always an improvement of a previous one. Whenever you compare the older version to the newer version, there is a difference. The new is always an improvement upon the old.

This tells us that as we change, we must aim to change for the better and not for the worst. This may encounter some draw backs or setbacks, but this is not to say that we will not change. Even if you stumble, you are still moving forward. Change helps us to understand the character and nature of God. Everything He made changes, with the exception of Himself. He is the Unchangeable Changer, meaning the God Who never changes but has the capacity to change everything.

God changes things

God changes things to transform destinies. In the book of Daniel, we find out that God is the author of times and seasons. He does this to regulate the world, including even the leaders of this world. Yes, both good and bad leaders are regulated by the King of kings.

And he <u>changeth</u> the times and the seasons: he removeth kings, and setteth up kings: he giveth wisdom unto the wise, and knowledge to them that know understanding: **Daniel 2:21 (KJV)**

Wisdom is a necessity to change and God gives it, so to positively change in your life or convert your gift, talents, and more, inquire from the Lord and you will have it. The Bible for instance is full of examples of how God made changes in the lives of people He wanted to transform to the next level.

In Genesis 17, God changed the name of Abram to Abraham, meaning the *"father of many."* Similarly, He changed the wife of Abram, Sarai, to Sarah (from *"my princess" to "princess"*). Again, Genesis 32 records how Jacob, who was originally known as the 'supplanter' or 'deceiver', wrestled with the Angel of the Lord to the point that his name was changed from Jacob to Israel, meaning *"one who struggles with God and overcomes"*.

In the New Testament, Jesus demonstrated the power of change when He changed people like Peter to Cephas, meaning *"stone"*. Saul on the road to Damascus also experienced a name change to Paul. These are symbolism of how God changes people's lives and destinies. What God did to these people's lives demonstrates to us that, the ability to change has the power and capacity to even depose limitation or curses or move a person from a negative situation to a positive one.

The problem today is that most people do not like or accept change. We do not understand the power of change. We seem not to understand that it is only in the maximisation of our abilities that success is guaranteed. Whenever a positive change occurs, it results in strength and power.

How to Make Relevant Changes: The Case of Jabez

The case of this young man's story is one that emphasises personal change as a key ingredient to multiplying what you have. You must be willing to make the necessary changes possible to ensure your next dimension. For you to make progress in life and enjoy what God has given you, you need to change the way you think or act, or your habits, character, etc., in order to affect your destiny.

These areas mentioned are the very key sensitive regions where most people fail and as a result need to be looked at spiritually and physically. If you do not like your personal circumstance now, then change. Be the change you want, because as Tony Robbins said, *"By not changing nothing, nothing changes."* A lot of people do want to change, but the big question still remains, *how do I change?* How do I apply this power or God-given ability to my life, circumstance, work or even family after so many years of developing negative habits and characters?

Now, the case of Jabez is one we all can identify with because it emphasises the fact that your life does not get better by chance, but by change and this can be effected through prayer. The truth is prayer changes everything, the negative situations or conditions, bad habits and characters. Your marriage, business and life can all be changed through prayer.

Jabez's quest to change also teaches us one of the major things this book seeks to emphasise, which is that we must be willing to change our course in order to live God's original purpose for our lives. He reminds us of the truth that God designed and provided keys and principles to change and keep us on purpose.

You have this ability to walk on courage to change, other than allowing crisis to change you. You can take stock of your life, redefine your vision and re-establish worthwhile goals. You can either let things happen or make things happen. It is your choice. As you study the famous prayer of Jabez, apply something to your life and work with God to fetch the necessary change your life needs.

> *"There was a man named Jabez who was more distinguished than any of his brothers. His mother named him Jabez because his birth had been so painful. 10He was the one who prayed to the God of Israel, "Oh, that you would bless me and extend my lands! Please be with me in all that I do, and keep me from all trouble and pain!" And God granted him his request."* ***1 Chronicles. 4:9-10 (NLT)***

To understand the power of change from this story, you must first:

1. Identify the area in your life you need change/multiply.

For Jabez, it was related to his name because names given at birth in Biblical times were big issues. His mother gave birth to him in pain and therefore gave him the name Jabez, which simply means pain.

While the young man was growing up, he was more honourable or distinguished than all his brothers but he probably found out that life was painful. Nothing he did was successful or he felt pain in everything he did. Why?

> "By not changing nothing, nothing changes."
> Tony Robbins

Because his name had taken possession of him and as a result was having impact on him.

In the same light, you may be more handsome, beautiful, and lovely than any member of your family, but some negatively developed habits, character, childhood, etc. can begin to affect your today if you do not begin to do something. You must begin to get involved to produce the quality of life you desire. Usually, the things that we need to change but do not change have the capacity to destroy and affect every facet of our being.

2. Work on the how. Prayer is key.

Once you have identified the area that needs changing, you then begin to work hard on the how. To Jabez, prayer was a key. We all need to consistently pray concerning issues in our lives but if your area of change involves taking pragmatic steps, then go ahead and do so because God has created you with this ability in your life and expects you to use it. It is only you who have the capacity to decide what you want. Doing nothing is no longer an option.

Jabez's quest for change is considered an ideal prayer because it is a demonstration of what could happen whenever you prepare to change from the negative to the positive. Bear in mind that your circumstance never changes until you do change. God does not respond to emotions but faith. He changes the negative circumstance you find yourself in by changing something about you first, and then your circumstances supernaturally begin to change. So there is something about you that first needs to change to alter your environment to bring about desired results.

His prayers were answered when he first experienced a name change. If you never depart from how you see yourself, you will never experience the reality that you have other possibilities.

Like Victor Frankl once said, *"When we are no longer able to change a situation, we are challenged to change ourselves."* And this is exactly what Jabez did.

His prayer depicts to us **three (3) key areas of possibilities** you can see in your life when you change.

1. Bless me:

The first prayer Jabez prayed was that 'God, change my name, not my situation, so that I can be blessed'. The only way you can be blessed out of a negative situation is by first changing the reason why you are not blessed now. Many at times people expect to be blessed without first changing something about them first.

> You can either let things happen or make things happen.

Repenting is therefore a key principle to releasing your blessing. Why? May be you cannot be blessed because of the situation you find yourself in. Your situation must change to accommodate your blessing. The truth is, something outside of you must change before you change.

The word blessed simply means "happy", a state of having through bliss. If your marriage, job or anything is not working presently, then stop blaming others or conditions for your unhappiness in life and start working to improve yourself and as you change, you will begin to see changes in your life.

2. Extends my lands.

His second prayer was 'Father, I need a name change so my lands or territories, business, career can be enlarged or extended'. What he meant was that life has limited him to pain and the only way to move into deeper and better uncharted territories was first to change from his negative situation, so he asked the Lord to help him.

> When we change, our level of influence increases and so does our ability to impact the world with what we have produced.

We all need to pray this prayer. Who does not need his or her level of influence to increase? Who does not want to multiply his fruits? We all do. Extend my land is simply a quest to increase one's level of influence. This is one of the possibilities of change. When we change, our level of influence increases and so does our ability to impact the world with what we have produced.

As a business owner, it is not until you become more resourceful, more diligent, more cooperative and creative in everything you do that you begin to experience growth in what you do. You cannot increase, grow or even develop what you have until you change.

The difference between where we are and mostly where we desire to be is mostly in the power to choose and change. This is why Chapters four and five are catalyst to multiplying and getting ready to replenish and subdue according to God's principles this book is emphasising.

Growth and development go through a process, a series of sequential actions to get to an expected end. For a child to grow, he goes through a process of crawling, standing, falling before walking and later running. When a child refuses to go through these processes of change, growth then becomes impossible.

Growth extends your land or level of influence. If you are not growing in life, then you are not experiencing true change. You need to be around people who appreciate growth so you can become who you were created to be. Development on the other hand involves applying pressure to ensure change. For instance, we all have muscles in our bodies, but for you to experience muscle development, you must be willing to hit the gym, eat extra good food and have plenty of rest to effect change.

This is what change involves. This may not be comfortable but it is always profitable to change for the better. Do not get it twisted. This is a principle that affects everything concerning your life and whole being as a human.

3. Be with me in all I do.

This is a prayer for the presence of God. God's divine presence is all you need in a world like ours. However, you cannot have Him while you are still living in sin and practicing your love affair with the world. If you want the supernatural to be with you, you have got to change from your old sinful ways, because the presence of God cannot dwell in sin. Usually, it is sin that takes us away from our source of blessings.

"Listen! The LORD is not too weak to save you, and he is not becoming deaf. He can hear you when you call. 2But there is a problem—your sins have cut you off from God. Because of your sin, he has turned away and will not listen anymore".
Isaiah 59:1-2 (NLT)

This verse confirms to us that there is a reason why life is difficult. It is not because God's hand is too short to reach out to you or His ears blocked from hearing your many prayers. It is your sins that are causing that. You cannot continue to stay in rebellion and expect His presence to be with or even go ahead of you

What makes people not to change?

Eric Hoffer was rightly on point when he said *"people will cling to an unsatisfactory way of life rather than change in order to get something better for fear of getting something worse."* In the midst of this great ability, we find out that people are unwilling to change. Change leads one to fulfil destiny, it brings blessings, growth and development, as the case studies of Jabez and others in this chapter have validated to us. However, the question still remains, why are people resistant to change?

> The moment you stop learning, you stop growing and where there is no growth and development, there ceases to be change.

Our focus at this point is to analyse some of the key reasons why most people refuse to change and how we can avoid them so as to move from quadrant one (fruit) to quadrant two (multiply).

1. Illusion of knowledge

This is one of the greatest obstacles to the ability to change. A position when people begin to feel they have finished learning or the feeling of 'I have arrived'. Sometimes, when you reach a level of training or attain a desired position, there is this temptation to slack off. For instance, it is very common that after a university education or a Master's programme, most people stop to read anything relevant for change.

The focus then becomes more on newspapers and celebrity magazines. Majority of men concentrate on the sports side of newspapers and majority of women dwell on celebrity magazines. This is a dangerous position to be in. The moment you stop learning, you stop growing, and where there is no growth and development, there ceases to be change. This feeling of you have arrived is what is causing no change in your life today.

Life is not learning for certificates and degrees, it goes beyond that. If you want to grow and change, you must be a person who seeks continual knowledge. Avoid the thinking that, I learn to gain a good job or career and after I have gotten the job, I stop learning. Over the years, I have developed a conscious, disciplined growth strategy, something for which I am grateful to my late father.

*While growing up, I had the mindset of going to school, getting certificate and getting a good job. So after school, I never read anything while at home, but my father kept on buying life-changing books and encouraging me to read and seek knowledge, but I refused. It was after my university education that one day while at home, I decided to pick one of my father's books and started reading. My intention was to at first please my old man. It was a John Maxwell's book on "**Be all you can be**" and I began to discover some life-changing principles.*

That was the beginning of growth, development and change in my personal life. I discovered that the most important things I needed to really succeed and live God's purpose for my life were not even in certificates and degrees but in the word of God. Since then, my life has never been the same and what you are reading now is a testimony to this fact.

So if you want to change, never stop learning. Read wide and seek wisdom from the word of God, which is the ultimate wisdom compared to what the world offers. This does not mean you should leave your primary or secondary education but rather that you should seek the wisdom to understand the difference.

"Wisdom is a principle thing, so get wisdom and in all your getting, get understanding" **Proverbs 4:7**

Philip Brooks, the Minister who spoke at Abraham Lincoln's funeral, asserted, *"sad is the day for any man when he becomes absolutely satisfied with the life he is living, the thought that he is thinking and the deeds that he is doing; when there ceases to be forever beating at the doors of his soul a desire to do something larger which he seeks and knows he was meant and intended to do."*

Never substitute anything for continual learning. You may have been fruitful in so many ways, but that is not enough. The purpose of this book again is to get you to understand that there is more to what you think you have produced. Move from productivity (fruit) to more productivity (multiply) to higher productivity (replenish) to greater heights (subdue).

2. Change changes routine

People do not want to change because of the long time habits they have developed. Over time, these habits become routine behaviours which then become very difficult to change. As a result of this, people find it difficult to give up and change.

There is a tendency to become addicted to routine stuffs such as non-nutritional drinks, alcohol, coffee, fizzy drinks and more. Television today has become one of people's idols of addiction. Some people are addicted to sin, pornography, fornication and adultery.

Notice that in this generation, when the Bible talks about not having any god with the exception of Jehovah God, He is usually talking about most of these things that take the place of God. The enemy knows that he cannot get you to go for one ugly piece of wood or stone to worship, but he can get you to be addicted to some negative routine habits such as mentioned in the earlier paragraph.

An addicted behaviour by its very nature is out of your control and usually takes more than your will to change. But you can decide to open your heart to the healing power of Christ to help you change. Changing from such routine behaviours involves a trade off and most of the time people are not ready to pay the price.

> Change is a personal determination.

To avoid a negative routine, you must evade anything that is producing a negative behaviour in your life. Avoid becoming a slave to anything but the Holy Spirit, the most important person on earth. It is far better to be intoxicated in the power of the Holy Spirit. He will teach you what to do, how to change and give you ability beyond your natural abilities. Be addicted to Him.

3. **People resist change because of traditional and cultural reasons**.

When we have ways of doing things that do not allow things to happen, it a sign that we must change. But most of the time, people do not change because of some cultural and traditional reasons.

You may not succeed in changing a whole generational tradition and cultural behaviour handed over from one generation to the other, but you can always succeed in changing yourself. Change is a personal determination. Remember, God usually does not change the problem first, He changes individuals and the surroundings automatically begin to change.

4. **People resist change simply because they do not want to pay the price of change**.

I mentioned earlier that there is always a trade off to change. To change here simply means you must be willing to give up something to gain a much more superior thing. But because you do not want to pay the price of change, then this ability will not be realised in your life.

> Never substitute anything for continual learning.

I remember writing my first book, "Alive for a Purpose". I used to write in the day time since I was not married when I started. After marrying and having children, things had to change if I were to continue writing. I have to now pay the price of waking up at ungodly hours after wife and kids have gone to bed in order to write.

Their needs come first during the day time and after they are settled, then I write. If I am not willing to pay this price, then I should bid my ability to move from quadrant one to two goodbye. However, as long as I am willing to make sacrifices by paying the price of change, then my gift and talent of writing can be multiplied in greater levels.

5. <u>Prayer</u>

When people fail to pray, they fail to change. Prayer is the single most effective change agent you possess. Yet many of us fail to use this 'weapon of mass destruction and construction'. God cannot help you if you do not pray. Do you know why? Because prayer is mainly what gives God the permission to interfere in earthly matters.

> When people fail to pray, they fail to change.

God originally created heaven for Himself and earth for us. This is mankind's greatest dominion; we are in charge of earth the same way God is of heaven. Do you know that no spirit can both enter and operate on planet earth without a physical body? This explains why the battle for your soul is between two kingdoms. Both the Kingdom of God and that of Satan need your permission to fulfill their purpose on earth. Whoever you give in to works through you. Is this not powerful? In fact, the womb of a woman is the only point of entry for anyone to enter earth. Even Jesus Christ needed the womb of a woman to come to earth. This shows the dominion mandate of you.

This is why prayer is such an important key, because it is the only thing that gives heaven license to operate on earth. It is our only mode of effective communication with our supernatural Father. Prayer is also our spiritual breathing, so when we stop praying, it is only a matter of time before we die, just as it is in the physical. One thing you will agree with me on is that dead people do not change.

To conclude this chapter, note that doing nothing is not an option, you must become an answer to your own prayer to change. The time has come that if we are to move to the next level with what we have, we must stop being content with our achievements and start developing strategies to change. Though change is inevitably our greatest challenge, God has given us the power alongside His help to fix things and walk in complete dominion.

APPLYING THE POWER OF CHANGE QUADRANT TWO PRINCIPLE (MULTIPLY)

1. **Growth=change**. Which area of your life, business, and family requires growth? To grow from fruit bearing to fruit multiplication, consider changes in the following areas if need be:
   - Environment   Friends
   - Thought process Character
   - Prayer life   Attitude
   - Books
2. Fact about change:
   - It is either you change or nothing changes
   - It is either you change or crisis will force you to change
   - You can either let things happen or make things happen
3. Two key principles that ensure changes that yield multiplied growth in life, business, ministry and career.
   - So begin today and take stock of your life, redefine your vision and re-establish worthwhile goals.
   - Be more resourceful, diligent, corporate and creative in your work, ministry or life.
4. How does this quote apply to your life? *"People will cling to an unsatisfactory way of life rather than change in order to get something better for fear of getting something worse."*
   Eric Hoffer
   - Have you substituted anything for continual learning?
   - Have you developed any long-term negative habits, such as addiction to alcohol or coffee; television, pornography or even fornication? Then consider ways to change from these if you want to multiply your productivity.

- ❖ Are you resisting change because of past track records or cultural reasons?
- ❖ Are you willing to trade off what you have for a greater and better tomorrow?
5. If you answer NO to many of these questions above, I encourage you to see a counsellor to seek help.
6. Seek to change because it leads you to fulfill destiny and to bring the blessing of growth and development.

QUADRANT THREE (REPLENISH)

THE POWER OF FOCUS

A focus concentration on what it takes…

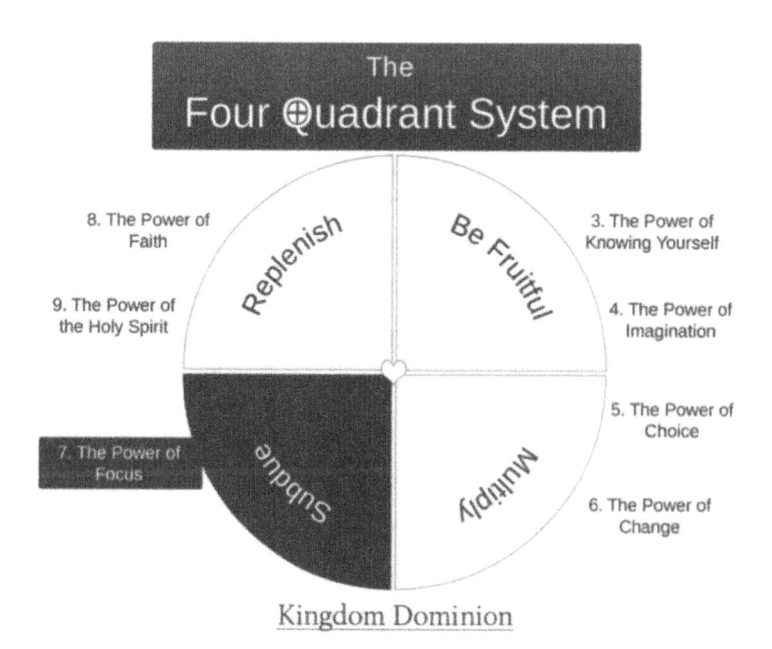

The Four Quadrant System

- 8. The Power of Faith
- 9. The Power of the Holy Spirit
- 7. The Power of Focus
- 3. The Power of Knowing Yourself
- 4. The Power of Imagination
- 5. The Power of Choice
- 6. The Power of Change

Quadrants: Replenish, Be Fruitful, Multiply, Subdue

Kingdom Dominion

7

THE POWER OF FOCUS

As an event photographer, I have the opportunity of working with different types of cameras. One of the fascinating features of every camera is its ability to focus. It is the focus of a camera that determines the quality of pictures you will give to your client. No matter how professional you may be in snapping an image, you need to first get the camera's focus right.

If the focus is right, your image will be good, but when the camera is out of focus, the final image will come out blurred. This is similar to the power of your focus. It is not only a camera that needs focus, your life needs focus too. As you read on the ability to focus, get ready to harness and maximise this all-important ability to succeed in your life and destiny.

> It is not only a camera that needs focus, your life needs focus too.

People fail most of the time not because they lack vision, ambition or even purpose, but because of lack of focus. Goals and visions provide energy sources to your life but to get the most out of your energy requires focus. We are distracted by a lot of things today. The system of the world is crumbling and the truth is those who put all their hope and focus on what is currently happening in this world get confused or side-tracked.

This chapter comes under **quadrant three,** which is about replenishment, primarily defined as *the ability to ensure that God given-seed (talents, passion) which has resulted into multiplied fruits continues in perpetuity. As multiplication breeds the increase, replenishment of your business, talents, ideas, and gifts breeds constancy and permanence.*

The purpose of this chapter is therefore is to help you to direct your endowed ability to focus on achieving constancy and permanence in what you have.

1. The word 'focus' is simply to direct your attention and attraction towards a planned activity or (a) set goal(s). At this level of the quadrant, in order to grow and develop, one must set life goals for business, product or even life. For life goals to be achieved, there must be annual goals and annual goals are reached through daily goals and this is where the power of focus plays a major part in achieving consistency and permanence in everything. As you focus on daily goals, you will reach annual goals and over time achieve life goals.

2. It is about declaring your intentions and taking specific strategies or plans to get results. The daily habits, attitude and strategy you focus on are what will determine replenishment over time.

3. Focus is the power behind having a purpose; without a clear focus on your purpose in life, nothing will be achieved.

4. It is about setting priorities around your purpose to ensure total energy and results. Consistency is not easy, but the more you learn to be consistent, the better you are to achieve

quadrant three and even four. The best well known businesses, churches, authors, musicians and more are those who are consistent in what they do.

You can be fruitful and multiply, but when you fail to be consistent, you will not be permanently known as you desire and this is why the power of focus is key.

Focus consists of **three** main processes necessary to help you replenish.

The first is **concentration**.

This is the ability to focus your mind on the main subject matter. When God created you, He gave you a tremendous ability to concentrate. Do you know that your mind receives thousands of stimuli or information daily but you have the power to focus on the main things? This is how powerful your ability to focus is.

In the midst of these, you have a tremendous ability to focus on God's purpose for your life. We live in a time where distraction is fast becoming the order of the day. One thing that kills your purpose in life is distraction and I believe this is one of the weapons of the enemy today to get people from focusing on the main things in life, thereby limiting potentials for reaching the highest level.

Today, you can be distracted by a lot of things or activities, from your past losses to current day's contemporary cultures such as T.V, jobs and more. That is why Paul in **Philippians 3:12-14 (NLT)** said,

"I don't mean to say that I have already achieved these things or that I have already reached perfection! But I keep working toward that day when I will finally be all that Christ Jesus saved me for and wants me to be. 13No, dear brothers and sisters, I am still not

all I should be, but I am focusing all my energies on this one thing: Forgetting the past and looking forward to what lies ahead, 14I strain to reach the end of the race and receive the prize for which God, through Christ Jesus, is calling us up to heaven."

This should be your attitude if you desire to win. You must use your ability to focus and concentrate all your energies on the main things in life because there will always be things to hinder progress in your life, but God has giving you this ability to focus and not be distracted.

> Comprehension is focusing on the knowledge of the truth.

The second process is **comprehension**.

This is the ability to focus on understanding, most importantly; you must choose to understand your main purpose in life and what you were born to do. Knowledge is good but not enough. This generation seeks lots of knowledge today but little comprehension. Do not get me wrong, knowledge is good but God expects us to do more with what we have.

Knowledge gives you information but comprehension helps you to understand the information you have. It is only after comprehension that one becomes empowered to apply knowledge and that is wisdom. This is why you are encouraged to "get wisdom but in all your getting, get understanding", because it is through comprehension a definite purpose is achieved, which is a key component to keep replenishing in your field of strength.

In the book of **John 8:32**, it reads *"you shall know the truth and the truth shall make you free"*. Comprehension is focusing on the knowledge of the truth. Notice that Jesus did not say you shall know alone, but rather know the truth. To know the truth involves understanding and you gain this by focusing on what you know, and only then can you begin to grow and develop.

The third process involves **meditation**.

The ability to ponder over something continuously over time. When your works, gifts and talents have yielded results and increased, continuous pondering of new ideas, new revelation and desire for new victories are the keys to ensuring replenishment. This is why God encourages us to meditate on nothing but His word, if only you want success. He told Joshua:

This book of the law shall not depart out of thy mouth; but thou shalt meditate therein day and night, that thou mayest observe to do according to all that is written therein: for then thou shalt make thy way prosperous, and then thou shalt have good success. Joshua 1:8 (KJV)

Meditation is your highest level of potency you can attain as a child of God and even with your secular and business activities. In the business world, meditation can be likened to reflection. At every stage in life, business or career, one must pause and reflect, take stock and develop new levels of thinking in order to move forward. This is what quadrant three (replenish) is all about. Pausing to meditate or reflect produces refreshment that provides new insights to continue.

> Pausing to meditate or reflect produces refreshment that provides new insights to continue.

It gets you to a different level effectively because nothing keeps your mind focused other than this spiritual discipline. In meditation or reflection, we see things from God's perspective. We focus on significance as we follow His lead. We are taught how to be humbled, for the key to going up is by first getting down.

Turning our attention back to Joshua (*from the book of Joshua*), you will discover that no other generation has achieved greatness beyond the Joshua generation, even up till today. The Joshua generation represents a generation, group, and organisation that:

a) **Displayed the power of God,**
b) **Destroyed demonic kingdoms and forces**
c) **Inherited the Promised Land**

Why? Because they did what the Lord instructed them in the verse above, and as a result God manifested himself before them like no other human being on the face of the earth has experienced.

"The Lord fought for Israel that day. Never before or since has there been a day like that one, when the Lord answered such a request from a human being." ***Joshua 10:14 (NLT)***

Now, let us turn our attention to some practical applications of the power and principle of focus.

Focus on Purpose.

Do you know that Jesus' life on earth depicted a high level of focus? Perhaps this explains his success level and the continuity of His legacy up till now. His leadership and principles still remain relevant to our current generation and he is therefore an example of what it means to replenish. This is a man who lived on earth for just 33 years but yet achieved the unimaginable.

He never built a building, but today, there are more buildings built for Him than any man on earth. What is His secret? Never in His life did He allow any unnecessary thing to distract Him from His calling; not worry, stress, depression or even anxiety. Through His life, He demonstrates to us the power of focusing on set priorities.

> *"The next morning Jesus awoke long before daybreak and went out alone into the wilderness to pray. 36Later Simon and the others went out to find him. 37They said, "Everyone is asking for you." 38But he replied, "We must go on to other towns as well, and I will preach to them, too, because that is why I came."* **Mark 1:35-38 (NLT)**

This man was always on point. His purpose was to preach, heal and set captives free and He did exactly that. Though everyone was asking for Him, the reason for His existence mattered to Him and He concentrated on that. In the same way, you can only accomplish much when you focus on your priorities and stay on purpose. To stay on purpose, one must also learn to get rid of things that so easily entangle, ranging from all manner of sin to unnecessary busy schedules or having one's day packed with activities.

> *And she had a sister called <u>Mary, which also sat at Jesus' feet, and heard his word</u>. 40But <u>Martha was cumbered about much serving</u>, and came to him, and said, Lord, dost thou not care that my sister hath left me to serve alone? bid her therefore that she help me. 41And Jesus answered and said unto her, Martha, Martha, thou art careful and troubled about many things: 42But one thing is needful: and Mary hath chosen*

that good part, which shall not be taken away from her. ***Luke 10:39-42 (KJV)***

In this example, you can learn that activity does not always equal success or achievement. Just because you are trying to do much in a day does not suggest that you will make it. There are not many things we all can do, only just a few, but in those few things we are capable of doing is the capacity to influence humanity if we can stick to them and continue in them. You need a focused concentration of what it takes to fulfill your goals.

> Activity does not always equal success or achievement.

While Mary focused on priority which is Jesus, Martha was getting herself entangled in doing many things at the same time. This will always result in much worry, depression, anxiety and most of the killer diseases destroying our generation today. One thing you can never make a mistake focusing on in life is the word of God. There is something better than feeling and that is the naked word of God.

There is a management principle called the 80/20 principle or the Pareto principle, named after **Vilfredo Pareto**, an Italian economist who discovered this in the 1906. This principle simply teaches that, when you focus your attention on the most important activities, you gain the highest return on your effort. Focusing on 20% of your most important priorities will yield 80% results.

For instance, Vilfredo Pareto observed that 20% of people in his country dominated 80% of the wealth. This is a principle and just as any principle can be applied in every area of your life, whether you are a child of God or a corporate executive, you cannot go wrong on this principle. It will work for you if you obey it and work against you when disobeyed. The choice is yours.

Examples of the 80/20 principle in our everyday life.

Workers: 20% of your staff produce 80% of your revenue, be it a business or church.

Leadership: 20% of the people make 80% of decisions

Wealth: 20% of the people control 80% of the world's wealth

Home: 80% of wear and tear on your clothes occurs on 20% of your clothes.

I have always seen a relationship between this principle and Jesus' feeding of the five thousand with just five loads of bread and two fishes. Figuratively, Jesus is teaching you the ability to accomplish much with the little that you have.

What do I focus on?

As you read about this God-given ability, it is important to know what you need to maximise this endowed power. A lot of people surely do want to focus on something worthwhile but often find themselves concentrating on weakness or what they lack in life. Admittedly, distraction has become the order of the day in this culture of ours.

In Chapter 1, I mentioned to you that one of the things your mind needs is focus. This is because we develop habits, whether positive or negative, as a result of the things we focus on. The mind is renewed by applying it to the things it focuses on.

For instance, if one is addicted to porn or drug abuse, such a person has developed such habit based on what he has focused on over the years. That is why Paul in **Philippians 4:8(NLT)** encourages us to focus on the right matter.

"And now, dear brothers and sisters, let me say one more thing as I close this letter. Fix your thoughts on what is true and honorable and right. Think about things that are pure and lovely and admirable. Think about things that are excellent and worthy of praise."

To begin with, focus on the **Word of God**.

Why? Because *"there is something better than feeling and that is the naked word of God"*–**Smith Wigglesworth**. If you depend on feelings, you will never develop and grow, so rather crave pure spiritual milk which is the word of God.. (**1 Peter 2:2**). Why? Because feelings do not develop faith but rather fear and weakness. It may be true you may not feel right, but you can still have faith if you focus on the word of God.

When you focus on the word, it becomes a lamp to your feet and a light to your pathway to success (Psalm 119:105). Your attitude key to living a holy and a sin-free life is through focusing on the word of God, and this is so important for the young people. (Psalm 119:9, 11).

> Life without a definite purpose is like your entire body system without a working spinal cord

Therefore, to replenish you must focus on:

1. Establishing a pattern of thinking:

All great men have a pattern of thinking they stick to over a long period of time. This is the key to steady and continuous progress. From Bible characters like Joseph, Moses, Daniel to modern names like Martin Luther King, Wright brothers and Steve Jobs.

Whatever the mind can conceive and believe, it can achieve and receive. Read the chapter on *the power of thought* in this book to learn more.

2. Establishing a definite purpose and vision.

Purpose is very important if you are to ensure replenishment. *Life without a definite purpose is like your entire body system without a working spinal cord.* All thriving business, ministry and organisation on this earth establish why they do what they do.

You may know what you do (**fruits**) and even how to do it very well (**multiply**), but if you do not know why you do it (**replenish**), there will be a problem. People do not buy what you do but why you do it and this is what will take you far. This is also what attracts people of like minds to your life, company or even ministry.

Vision on the other hand is a clear mental picture of a better tomorrow given by God. I like the definition of **George Barna** who said, "*Vision is a foresight, based on an insight with the benefit of hindsight.*" This simply means vision is seeing where you are meant to be from where you with no distractions.

When God gives you a vision, concentrate on it. Let nothing move you. Always give yourself fully to that vision and it shall come to pass. As vision grants you a picture of tomorrow, purpose guarantees the success of today to make tomorrow's mental picture a reality over time.

3. Values: These are what guide your vision and purpose. They are the things you cherish and as a result hold dearly to your heart. They are internal and subjective and represent our strongest feelings thereby guiding our behaviour. When we put values and principles together, we get value principles. We can get results today and even greater results in the future when these two work effectively in our lives and work.

These two work better because, while values are internal, principles are external laws that govern our actions. So values govern our behaviour while principles again govern our actions, which is the consequence of our behaviour. This together becomes a powerful tool for replenishing what you have already achieved or produced.

> When we put values and principles together, we get value principles

4. Priority: set priorities in your life and focus on them. These are the key things in your life you plan to do. Not everything carries the same value. Things of most importance should not be met with least attention. To begin with, let your vision and purpose become your priorities in life

In sorting out your priorities, John Maxwell proposes three key questions I recommend to you. Let these questions take center stage of your desire for replenishing what you have.

1. Requirement: *what is required of me?* In Acts 9:6, when Christ met Paul on his way to Damascus, what we now refer to as the Damascus experience, Paul asked one simple but defining-moment question, *what will thou have me do?*

You too should have your Damascus experience. It is a point of yielding and yielding until you discover something worthwhile to focus on. It is again the point of submitting yourself before God and indeed yourself and obeying what you are required to do.

When Paul yielded to this question and knew what was required of him, he wasted no time in focusing on his priorities. No wonder he accomplished much in his purposeful life.

II. Results: *what gives you the most results?* You should spend most of your time on the things that give you the greatest results in your life. This is simple wisdom. There are areas of your strength and weakness. It is your responsibility to decide whether to focus on your strength or weakness area. Focus on what gives you most results in life.

III. Rewards: *what gives you most rewards?* Not all areas give you the same results. To move from fruit production and fruit multiplication to fruit replenishment, one must focus on areas that yield rewards.

5. Establishing continuous innovation:

Let me ask you, why do you think that majority of people in this day and age of technology will choose one company's product over others? Be it smart phones, computers, televisions and more. This is usually not because such companies have they been fruitful and multiplied over the market, but they have continuously stayed innovative over the years. It is as if they lead and the rest follow.

From his speech on TED.com on *"how great leaders inspire action"*, Simon Sinek argued from the *Law of diffusion* of innovation which states that:

- ❖ 2 ½ % of our population are our innovators (replenish).
- ❖ 13 ½ % of our population are our early adaptors.
- ❖ 34 % of our populations are majority.

Judging from this research, it means that there is a lot of work to be done to increase the population of our innovators (replenish). This also shows that the higher we go in the process of achieving these mandated quadrants, the

> People do not buy what you do but why you do it and this is what will take you far.

more men drop down the ranks. Majority of people bear fruits, but the number of those that actually multiply reduces significantly and even becomes lower than the number of those who continuously replenish and subdue.

There comes a stage in your career, business or ministry that it is not just fruitfulness that will sustain you but your ability to remain relevant to the environment, society and world with changing contingencies. This is why as things change; you must develop new ways of thinking that will ensure your consistency and continuity at the top.

Stop looking for motivation from man because it is not always from man that you will find motivation. Stop looking for inspiration from things you can see and touch, as things you will see sometimes may not inspire you. Get up daily with a focus on Jesus, the author and finisher of life and develop the discipline that will keep you growing. **Michael Angier** puts it this way, *"if you develop the habits of success, you will make success a habit."*

Finally, a focus concentration on a PLAN is key to your fulfillment of quadrant three(3).

*P*repare to focus

*L*aunch out your purpose.

*A*djust as you move.

*N*etwork with the right people.

This simple procedure can be a very useful tool when followed. As you concentrate on these principles, you will replenish what you have produced and multiplied.

APPLYING THE POWER OF FOCUS QUADRANT 3 PRINCIPLE (REPLENISH)

1. The chapter begins with the idea of achieving quadrant three (replenish)–your productivity. To do this, you need everything in quadrant one and two plus this chapter. You cannot replenish (ensure consistency and continuity) in your life until you produce and multiply your fruits.

2. What life goals have you set for your life, career, business, family or even ministry? Life goals are achievable only when broken into annual goals and annual goals broken down to daily goals. Focusing on daily goals = achieving consistency (replenishment).

3. What do you intend to do with your life, business, profit and what strategy have you got to do it?
   - **Concentration: Ability to focus on primary purpose and stay on priority**
   - **Comprehension: Is your ability to understand what you do, why you do it and how to do it.**
   - **Meditation /Reflection: It provides new insights to reinvent yourself in areas of replenishment.**

4. Consider the Pareto Principle by Vilfredo Pareto and apply it to your life. The principle simple states that focusing on 20% of your priorities will yield 80% results.

5. What drives you in life? Is it your
   - **Possession or lack?**
   - **Strength or weakness?**
   - **Success or failure?**
   - **Faith or fear?**

Quadrant 3 Principle (Replenish)

Your attitude key to success is to be consistently and constantly driven by what you have, strength, success, faith and opportunities ahead.

6. Finally, to replenish:
   I.   Establish a pattern of thinking
   II. Establish a definite purpose and vision
   III. Develop clear cut values
   IV. Set values: Put first things first

In setting values, follow John Maxwell's 3 key stages:
- **Focus on what is required of you**
- **Focus on what yields the greatest results**
- **Focus on what gives you the most rewards**
- **V   Establish continuous innovation. Apply the law of diffusion of innovation**

Like Michael Angier said, "If you develop the habit of success, you will make success a habit" All the best.

QUADRANT FOUR. (SUBDUE)

THE POWER OF FAITH

Going beyond the evidence.

"Skill and confidence are an unconquered army."
George Herbert

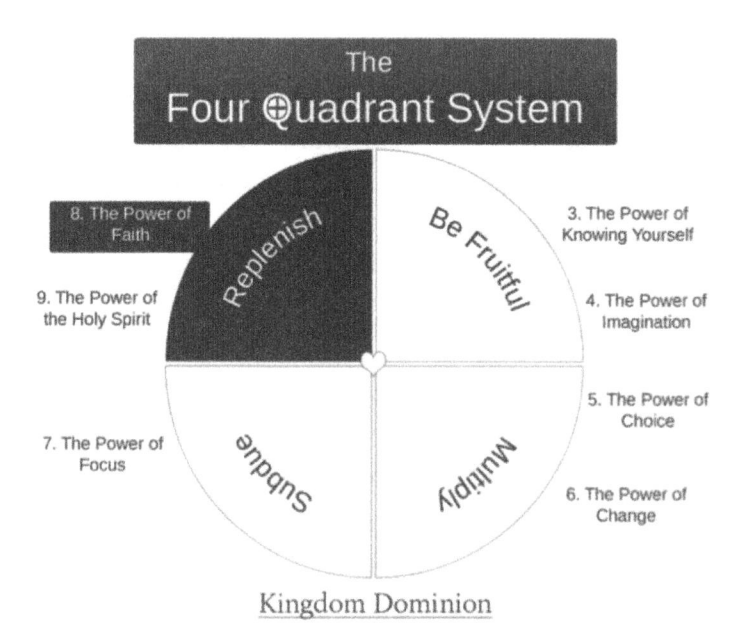

8

THE POWER OF FAITH

In the next two chapters, you will discover two key greater abilities that have capacity to change you to walk in complete kingdom dominion for your life, business and ministry. It is important to note that as you strategise to replenish your success and victory at this level, you will be faced with even deeper and stronger challenges. It is in your ability to overcome stronger hurdles in life that total or complete dominion is attained.

This is where the fourth quadrant (subdue) becomes necessary. Again, observe that God's commandment to man is to be fruitful, multiply, replenish and subdue. This means that to walk in complete dominion involves subduing.

> Life is like a wrestling competition. It is not until you wrestle and defeat major opponents that you become a champion.

You have not totally walked in dominion until you have subdued. As already defined from Chapter One, to subdue is *to conquer, overcome or bring under control by either physical or spiritual force.* The word 'subdue' originally comprises two words joined together, when observed carefully. These are **'sub'** and **'due'**. **'Sub'** has to do with putting something under your feet, whereas **'due'** simply imply timing.

To put the two definitions together gives us a perfect meaning of what it means to subdue. As endowed as we are to walk in dominion, success and victory, there will always be times that we have to put under our feet opposing forces (physically and spiritually) that will threaten our destinies and organisations. Life is like a wrestling competition. It is not until you wrestle and defeat major opponents that you become a champion. This is how the fourth quadrant is illustrated in the Bible.

" *¹¹ Put on the whole armour of God, that ye may be able to stand against the wiles of the devil.¹² For we wrestle not against flesh and blood, but against principalities, against powers, against the rulers of the darkness of this world, against spiritual wickedness in high places.*" **Ephesians 6:11-12**

To withstand these physical and spiritual attacks, we must depend on God's strength and every piece of God's armour to ensure dominion. This is why the purpose of this chapter and the next is to reveal to you two key weapons needed to fight and achieve complete victory. These two are **faith** and the **Holy Spirit's power**. Now from this point, we will reveal the power of faith.

We cannot speak on abilities and divine enablement without speaking on the power of faith. The greatest ability of all is this ability and it is my prayer that, as you continue to read this book, God will grant you the special strength to bring this glorious power into your life.

Walking in dominion cannot be possible if we refuse to walk in faith/confidence. There is a level of belief one must exhibit to bear fruit and an even deeper faith to demonstrate if you are to multiply, replenish and subdue. Nothing ventured, nothing gained.

> Every one of us has more faith than we are currently using.

Every one of us has faith, yet not all of us have activated this ever-increasing power in God, which is one of His gifts to all mankind. Let me expound on the last line a bit more. There are two kinds of faith. All men have been born with a *natural faith*. This is why every human being has a level of faith that still works for him/her in different areas of life.

This kind of faith looks at what we can see and handle.

Secondly, there is the God kind of faith/confidence. God calls us to His kind of confidence, which is His gift to us. Human/natural faith can fail but faith in God never fails. This is the kind of faith I want to introduce you to, because the truth is, every one of us has more faith than we are currently using.

The God kind of faith/confidence is one that can move mountains and go beyond your natural order. Our natural faith has limitations and can come to an end. There is a point man gets to and hits the ceiling, whether in life or even in a business organisation, yet the faith in Christ Jesus can help and take us beyond. The kind of faith that begins to see God as the foundation and His word a standing you can depend on is what it means to operate like a champion.

God has something to give you but the only way to receive it is through faith and nothing else, *for without faith it is impossible to please God* (**Hebrews 11:6**). For there to be breakthroughs, progress and direction in your life, you must begin to walk on the lines

The Power Of Faith

of this increasing ability, because this is the only way to all of God's treasures.

> *For twenty five years, one man (Abraham) dared to activate this power of faith in God in his life. This means that every day for twenty five years, he looked up to God to do what He had promised him. God had promised him a son and called him out of his family and friends.*
>
> *You will bear witness with me that if his faith came from man, he would have been tired, but because he believed in God, he kept going. On one hand, there was Sarah his wife, growing old and weaker by the day and he was not getting any younger either. Yet The Bible says, when there seemed not to be hope, Abraham believed in hope, unwavering concerning the promise of God* **(Genesis 12:1-3, Romans 4: 17-23)** ***emphasis added.***

Now this is faith, *the ability to hold true the Word of God, no matter what happens or does not happen.* No wonder Abraham has become the father of this ability. If this man could believe and not waver, then God is using his life to teach us too

❖ **How old is your issue?**

❖ **What is that problem that causes you to worry and fear?**

The key is faith. Everything happens by this ability, including the grace that leads us into salvation. **Romans 4:16 (KJV)** says this, *"Therefore it is of faith, that it might be by grace; to the end the*

> This power of faith is the basis of everything.

promise might be sure to all the seed; not to that only which is of the law, but to that also which is of the faith of Abraham; who is the father of us all,"

Notice the first line of the verse confirming what is being spoken. *Therefore it is of faith that it might be by grace.* This means that I cannot have the grace of God without faith. What therefore is Grace? *Grace is an unmerited favour. Something you have not laboured for but gained access to.* This means that your ability to be fruitful, multiply, replenish and subdue can be defined as grace or unmerited favour simply because they have been prearranged for you by God. Therefore, fulfilling your kingdom dominion mandate at each level requires faith.

Thus, you cannot bear fruits without first believing in the seeds you sow, neither can you multiply your fruits without faith and, most importantly, there can never be continuity (replenishment) and overcoming forces (subdue) without this faith.

On a more serious note, to ensure success at each level of these principles, you need to exercise even much greater faith if you want to experience complete dominion. The confidence it takes to bear fruit needs to increase to multiply your productivity and you need to have even stronger confidence to keep replenishing and subduing.

This is why I reserve this chapter and beyond for those who are perusing the third and fourth quadrant, because many individuals, businesses, organisations and even ministries have no doubt succeeded in fruitful ventures but have failed in ensuring continuity and overcoming challenges over the years.

Faith therefore is like a door that one must open for God's grace to usher in. God is first and ever ready to come in but the question is, are you ready to open the gates of your heart to Him (Rev

3:23), because the gateway to your heart can only be opened through this power and enablement This ability is accordingly defined in **Hebrews 11**, which is also known as the *"Hall of faith"* because it contains the accounts of men and women who ventured into greatness with this ability of walking in kingdom dominion.

"Now faith is the substance of things hoped for, the evidence of things not seen. **Hebrews 11:1 (KJV)**

What a powerful piece of scripture only if you can believe! Now faith is a **substance,** yet this substance we are talking about here cannot be looked at, handled, touched or Felt. It is greater than what we can see. This substance does not appeal to human reasoning or wisdom, yet it has the capacity to handle you.

Everything we see in the natural is fading or shall one day fade away. The cars, money, houses, clothes, you just name them. I call these *fake substances*; yet, that which you cannot see, which is more real than you, is the substance of all things which God is trying to explain to us.

To understand this in relation to fulfilling your dominion mandate, observe with your eyes, how God through the power of faith demonstrates this fourth quadrant.

*"Through faith we understand that the worlds were framed by the **word of God**, so that things which are seen were not made of things which do appear."* **Hebrews 11:3 (KJV)**

"For you have been born again. Your new life did not come from your earthly parents because the life they gave you

will end in death. But this new life will last forever because it comes from the eternal, **living word of God.** "**1 Peter 1:23 (NLT)**

"In the beginning was **the Word**, *and the Word was with God, and the Word was God. (v14) And* **the Word** *was made flesh, and dwelt among us, (and we beheld his glory, the glory as of the only begotten of the Father,) full of grace and truth."* **John 1:1, 14 (KJV)**

All things we see were created from things we cannot see and this is the substance of faith. One underlined word uniting all these remarkable verses is the Word of God. *This substance (faith) is the word of God. It is God's treasure from heaven, which resides in you holding God's power for your life.* God is our foundation and the Creator of everything; His Word is our standing and possesses creative abilities.

The words you speak over your life, family, business and ministry have creative abilities. If you are to move successfully from bearing fruit to subduing strongholds in every facet of life, then you must be careful of what you say and how you mean it. Faith is simply what I say and do. Indeed, the door to the supernatural hangs on these two things.

First, your belief and secondly what you speak. *"¹³ We having the same spirit of faith, according as it is written, I believed, and therefore have I spoken; we also believe, and therefore speak;"* **2 Corinthians 4:13 (KJV)**

> The level of faith you carry will always be equal to the level of victory you will achieve.

Because this substance cannot be seen or handled, the only way to lay hold of it is through Hope. So the first sentence of Hebrews 11 concludes like this, "Now *faith is the substance of things hoped for"*. *Hope is your confident expectation.* One thing that precedes faith is hope because it prepares you to walk in this substance of faith and brings what is not into being.

Your faith will never move beyond the question mark.

There are two things about hope you should hold on to; *hope does not give up neither will it disappoint you.*

Let me share this true story with you. *Two men met in prison and became friends. One day as they were chatting together, friend (**A**) said to friend (**B**) that though everything had been stripped away from him, he still had <u>hopes</u> to one day come out of prison and still make it in life.*

*Knowing very well that friend (**A**) was serving back-to-back life sentences, friend (**B**) quickly told (**A**) to shut up because hope was a dangerous thing for a man in his state. Now, it so happened that after 16 years, friend (**A**) was released and went out to become very rich as he had told his friend. It also came to pass after 30 years that friend (B) was let out of his life sentence for good behavior and destiny brought these friends together again. Friend B was surprised to see how successful and rich his friend had become. What he hoped for had become a reality.*

Precious one, I believe we can all learn from this story. For 16 years, a man chose to hold on to hope without giving up and this hope did not disappoint him. This is what this substance of faith is all about. Note that what he hoped for while in prison was not seen or handled for all that long time, yet after a period of 16 years, total kingdom dominion became a reality. Let this true story apply to you.

What is that prison, problem, limitation or issue you find yourself in today? Know that *faith is the substance of things hoped for, the evidence of things not seen.*

Faith can also be defined simply as victory. It is the victory that overcomes our prison, problems, pains, fears and brings into action all of God's principles within our hearts, which is your dominion mandate. Here in lies the truth; the level of faith you carry will always be equal to the level of victory you will achieve.

> *"For whatsoever is born of God overcometh the world: and this is the victory that overcometh the world, even our faith."*
> **1 John 5:4 (KJV)**

The great Harvard psychologist and philosopher **William James** coined the term *"Precursive faith"*, which explained is the faith that runs ahead of the evidence. This is similar to what the Bible teaches. We all need precursive faith to overcome our fears and limitations.

Smith Wigglesworth, a man known as the Apostle of Faith in our generation, defines this faith as *a deep reality caused by God's personality waking up our humanity to leap into eternal things and be lost forever in something a million times greater than yourself.* All that Smith is saying is that, to understand this kind of ability (faith) and its impact over your life, business, family or even career, you must first of all step out from human thinking, where the emphasis is on what we can see or touch in order to determine what is possible or impossible, and leap into God's ways of making things a deeper reality.

For instance, it is impossible for man to understand God and His creation process if we do not step into His personality; only then can we have knowledge of eternal things and their impact over us.

You must value nothing more highly than your faith, because it is the one major currency you need to move through the pattern of your dominion mandate. Nothing happens without faith. There is no great man, family, business organisation and certainly no thriving ministry without faith.

One of the major components of why great men or organizations fall from grace to grass is the lack of faith/confidence. Research into some of the major losses this world has ever seen and you will discover that somewhere along the line, somebody or people failed to move by faith. **Mother Teresa** said *"faith keeps the person who keeps the faith"* so find faith and let faith keep you.

Proving your faith

You do not believe in something until it is truly tested and, in fact, nothing is yours until it stands the ordeal of time. The option of confidence is living because without confidence, you will easily give up. The pattern of walking in dominion consists of processes which surely include testing and proving our faith at each level or quadrant. This is the formation of values and action guidance, meaning faith/confidence must be an intrinsic part in what you cherish to lead your actions.

For there to be fruits in life, your faith will be tested, and to move from just yielding results to multiplying, replenishing and subduing from quadrant one (fruitful) involves deeper and harder tests. The secret to reaching your fullest potential, especially achieving the fourth quadrant (subdue), is in a series of tests you pass along your walk into dominion. The moment you stop proving your confidence at each level is the moment you fail. *For instance, as an author, the moment I stop developing continuous strategies to market and get my books across the world is the moment I fail at the third quadrant* (replenish).

'What level are you?' and 'how are you proving your faith?' are therefore important questions you have to answer now. It is either God will test you or use the devil to prove your faith no matter who you are or what you do. Your life will constantly be tested, so will your business and practically everything you represent.

One key thing Satan is after is your faith because faith is your currency for purchasing your dominion mandate and forms the basis of fulfilling all the quadrants. Another key purpose in this chapter is not only to move you deeper into the God kind of faith but also to warn you from failing in faith, especially in the process and pattern of your dominion mandate. If you doubt this, check the life of Job. This man's life, family and business were tested to the highest level and he passed. No wonder twice as much blessing than he had before was added to him at the end.

The devil will test your faith in five (5) levels or ways you need to be aware of. I fondly call these the **five (d's)** of the devil.

1) Doubt:

One of the key proofs of your confidence comes through doubt. You do not believe in something until you first doubt it. *"The honor of the conquest is rated by the difficulty."* **Michel de Montaigne**. Doubt is the enemy to your manifestation. At each level of your dominion mandate, the enemy will bring fear, frustration and worry across your way to stop you from progressing. As prayer is a prerequisite to fulfilling your dominion mandate, it is important you pray in faith and not doubt, because many pray and yet doubt the power and potency of prayer.

Operating especially in the third and fourth quadrants most times consists of defying facts and walking in the truth. For instance, the fact that you are finding it difficult to breakthrough in life, business or even ministry does not change the truth that you can overcome. You must learn to remove roadblocks from your life because in life, if you do not do so, your confidence will never move beyond the question mark. Learn to move yourself from Doubt Street to Faith Victory Street.

2) Diversion

Another one of the devil's tactics is to divert your attention as you make efforts to progress through the quadrants. The key aim is to get you to lose focus on the main things, especially in areas of your weakness rather than strength. However, to be successful, you have to learn to focus on what you can do and not what you cannot do. In concentrating your thoughts on the main things,

- **A. Do not think like everyone else does.** Be unique in your thinking process. I therefore charge you to always be different. Do not take everything you see or hear around you inside of you. Just because a thought comes to you does not mean you have to think it. In short, be careful about your thought patterns.
- B. **C. Focus like a lion eating a prey.** Be careful of the noise and shouts around you. Decide never to allow anything to break your focus, because a lot of challenges will come your way to stop you, especially in the third and fourth quadrants.

"⁴But this is what the Lord has told me: "When a strong young lion stands growling over a sheep it has killed, it is not frightened by the shouts and noise of a whole crowd of shepherds, it just goes right on eating". **Isaiah 31:4** (NLT)

There is a reason why God identifies Himself with these two animals in the world: the lion and the eagle. This is because of their nature and the behaviour and character they exhibit. The lion may not be the strongest, biggest, smartest in the jungle, yet it can kill an elephant. It is called the king of the jungle. Why? Because of the faith and confidence it carries.

> Faith is not a technique, a method or a science but a way by which kingdom mindset is developed.

Both the lion and eagle possess qualities that subdue and make it to the fourth quadrant. In the same light, the person or organisation that wants to make it to the top must have a lion or an eagle mentality. Both of these animals have what we call attitude and attitude is a product of faith or belief. Faith is therefore not a technique, a method or a science but a way by which kingdom mindset is developed.

D. Stand on the Word of God always. As a matter of truth, eat the Word of God. Even Jesus before he began his public ministry was tempted to lose focus. It only took the power of God's Word to keep him intact. The best way is to practice **focus thinking,** i.e. *the ability to remove distraction and mental clutter in order to concentrate with clarity,* through feeding on God's Word.

> "Have patience, everything is difficult before they become easy". Persian poet Saadi

> *"But Jesus told him, (Devil)* "No! The Scriptures say 'People do not live by bread alone, but by every word that comes from the mouth of God" **Matthew 4:4 (NLT)**

3) Delay

Another tactic of the enemy to get you to lose faith is by delaying things in your life. Growing and moving through the levels of the quadrants may sometimes prolong success but you must be careful not to lose faith. Patience is a virtue you need to develop when projects seem to be prolonged. Be patient and value every process along the way to the top.

Persian poet Saadi said, *"have patience, everything is difficult before they become easy"*. The people who want to taste complete dominion must harness the power of patience and persistence alongside being motivated and consistent daily, for motivation will get you going forward while consistency will ensure growth. Always remember that everything worthwhile in life always takes dedication and time. Delay does not necessarily mean denial, so be strong and never lose your faith. *"Endure and persist; this pain will turn to your god by and by."* Ovid

> *"This vision is for a future time. It describes the end, and it will be fulfilled. If it seems slow in coming, wait patiently, for it will surely take place. It will not be delayed."* **Habakkuk 2:3 (NLT)**

However, a word of caution to the one waiting; to wait is not to put up with, or remain idle, as usually implied. Just as a teacher teaches, a singer sings, a dancer dances and a driver drives, so it is that a waiter/waitress waits (serves). I used this analogy to prove to you that, to wait is simply to serve, and as defined already, service (wait) is the rent you pay for what you seek to enjoy or benefit.

> The day you stop needing encouragement is the day you cease to exist.

4) Defeat: Many have failed and made failure their final destination in life. How sad when you allow the enemy to use defeat, mistakes and errors as a tool to steal 'like precious faith' from you. However, the truth is you are not the only person who has failed at the level you ought to be. Do you agree with me that those who fulfil their dominion mandate have all failed before?

The question therefore is *what makes / made the difference?* It is their faith never to give up but use their defeat to still carve success for themselves. Begin to see failure as a sign of progress and rather than give up and distance yourself from the experience, forge ahead and ask the right questions that will help you to subdue things under your feet. It is even in the hard or needy places that God chooses to show His power.

"We are pressed on every side by troubles, but we are not crushed. We are perplexed, but not driven to despair. ⁹ We are hunted down, but never abandoned by God. We get knocked down, but we are not destroyed." ***2 Corinthians 4:8*** *(NLT)*

5) Discouragement

Instead of comfort, there may be affliction from every direction; but fear not, for God will send destiny helpers to encourage you. One of the key mechanisms the enemy uses along the route to your dominion mandate is discouragement and this is aimed at your faith and nothing else. Discouragement therefore is a faith destroyer and things will always happen just to discourage you. Do you know that even after enjoying major victories along the way the enemy will tempt you with discouragement?

As discouragement disables, encouragement enables you. To succeed at every level of the quadrants, encouragement is a key factor every day. It breathes new life and possibilities into your life. It is not something you need sometimes but all the times and seasons of your life on earth. The day you stop needing encouragement is the day you cease to exist. It is the anchor to the faith that makes things happen. The keys to being encouraged are the following:

1. God's Word: The most potent source of encouragement is no doubt the Word of God. When nothing will encourage you, trust me, God's Word will do. *"But David encouraged and strengthened himself in the Lord his God"*, **1 Samuel 30:6 (AMP);** David is just one example of the many who made the Word of God their source of encouragement. I do not know what you believe but no matter who you are, God's Word, beyond any reasonable doubt, is a fountain you can drink from. *"Faith comes by hearing and the message is heard through the Word of God."* **Romans 10:17**. Try it today.

> As discouragement disables encouragement enables.

2. Speak Life: The words you speak or allow to be spoken to you can generate encouragement or discouragement. It is your choice, however; always speak life no matter your situation or circumstance. Speak life to your family, marriage, career, ministry, finances consistently and watch your life grow from fruitfulness through to subduing forces under your feet.

3. Be a source of encouragement to others: Be determined to be an encourager to someone each day. The secret is, as long as you become a source of encouragement to others, you yourself will never lack faith. Somebody once told me and I also write to you: be like the pipe that always allows water to flow through it, for such pipe shall never get rid of water. You are a channel of blessing to somebody, don't block the road.

Character

Finally, just as *William James*, 'The greatest discovery of my generation is that, humans can alter their lives by altering their character of mind.' In order words, you need a high level character to sustain you at this level of the quadrants and it is your faith that will produce the character it takes to keep rising.

Now you may ask, what role will the right character play in my life, business, career, ministry and more at quadrant four? Permit me to spell out seven reasons why you need the faith that produces the right character and attitude.

1. Character is the moral core of every person. *Philippians 2:5-7*
2. Character is destiny.
3. Character is that ingredient which sustains what you attain.
4. Character is the major difference between success and failure. *Numbers 13-14, 1 Samuel 17*
5. Character is what gives you uncommon perspective on life. *Philippians 4:8, Proverbs 23:7*
6. Character is either your best friend or worst enemy.
7. Character is what determines action and action determines achievement.

When we refer to a person's moral core, we refer to his moral characteristics or tendencies which either produces good results or bad results. Just look below at what by your faith, courage or confidence at this level, one can produce great results and without it, one can lose out and fall off the quadrants.

<u>Good Character verses Bad Character</u>
1. Good Character breeds dreams.
   Bad character breeds disappointment.
2. Good character starts building.
   Bad character starts blaming.
3. Good character gets busy.
   Bad character gets angry.
4. Good character conquers.
   Bad character quits.

Where do you want to be? Make your pick. It takes confidence, courage and faith beyond the evidence to succeed at quadrant four.

APPLYING THE POWER OF FAITH
QUADRANT FOUR (SUBDUE)

1. To achieve success or dominion at this level, you need all in quadrant one (fruitful) plus quadrant two (multiply) plus quadrant three (replenish) before what is being taught at this level can become relevant. This is the interdependent nature of God's first commandment to mankind.
2. Develop a winning mentality by holding on no matter what happens or does not happen. Your attitude is key to subduing challenges and obstacles in life and business.
3. Recognise that the power of Faith is the basis of everything. Everything begins and perpetuates by faith. Believe in God and in what He has given you.
4. All things were created and made through the Word of God spoken on earth. In the same light, you in God's image can begin to subdue by continuously speaking life not death over your life, marriage, children, business, etc., no matter what the problems, challenges or even obstacles are.
5. The higher you go in the four quadrants, the higher your faith/confidence will be tested.
   - **In what ways are you therefore proving your faith?**
   - **Are you giving up or still fighting?**
   - **What is the one thing which, if you do it, can make a difference in your life, business or ministry?**
6. Your greatest enemy is the devil and to prove your faith, watch out for the 5 dangers of the devil: **Doubt, Diversion, Delay, Defeat, Discouragement**
7. Overcome and fulfil quadrant 4 (subdue) by:
   - **Encouraging yourself with the Word of God**
   - **Learning to constantly speak life to yourself, business and more.**
   - **Being a source of encouragement to others.**

QUADRANT FOUR (SUBDUE)

THE POWER OF THE HOLY SPIRIT

The fire that drives everything

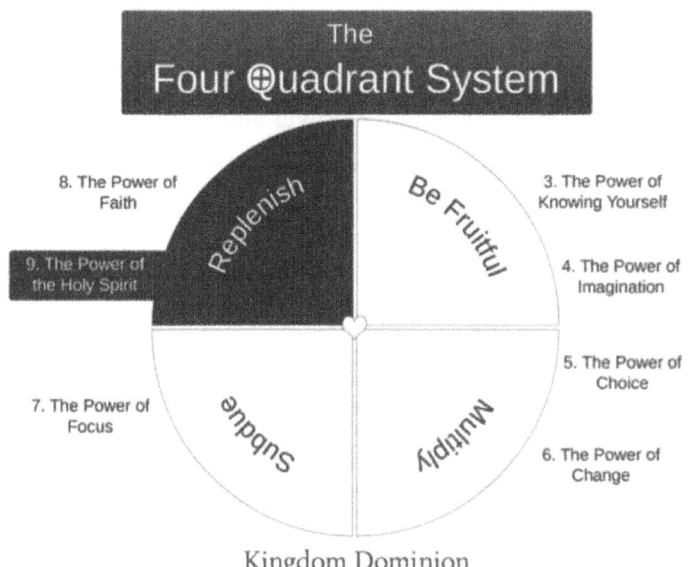

9

THE POWER OF THE HOLY SPIRIT

This chapter introduces you to a different level of ability. God has endowed you with potentials, power and solutions, yet there is a limit to what man can do and achieve. However, to go beyond your endowed abilities and rest assured of winning in every aspect of your life, you must yearn for this all-important ability.

This chapter comes under the **fourth quadrant,** which is to subdue. From the introductory chapter, to subdue is *to conquer, overcome or bring under control by either physical or spiritual force*. The Holy Spirit is the third person of the Trinity that also includes God the Father and God the Son. The anointing is the manifestation of the personality of the Holy Ghost.

So, in this chapter you will discover more about the Holy Spirit as a Person and His personality, which manifests the anointing, and how He is key to achieving the fourth quadrant (subduing). The Holy Spirit has all the qualities belonging to a person. He has the power to understand, to will, to do, to call, to change, to empower, to hear and to love.

> The anointing is an increasing force, an enlargement in a believer.

The Power of the Holy Spirit

The anointing is a divine enabler that comes from God the Holy Ghost. Gaining this power is simply inheriting God's 'super' on your 'natural' or His 'extra' on your 'ordinary' to do the supernatural and the extraordinary. In fact, according to **Isaiah 10:27**, the anointing is a yoke destroyer and a burden remover. Thus, where this ability is operating, you will triumph so much that, whatever problem you are facing will be destroyed and removed. It will break every stress, depression and worry. The anointing is an increasing force, an enlargement in a believer.

The Holy Spirit and His power remains the most important ability you must yearn for today because He remains the governor of God's Kingdom according to **Isaiah 9:7**.

> The anointing is a yoke destroyer and a burden remover.

Secondly, He is here to finish the work God the Father and God the Son started. These are some of the reasons why there is so much emphasis on Him and what He has to offer to your life.

My reason for getting you interested in this ability is because He is a person whose personality is bigger and better than yours so when He operates in your life, business and ministry, everything becomes successful. As Jesus represents the Word of God, the Holy Spirit is the power of God. In **1 John 2:27**, the anointing can also be referred to as the unction of the Holy Spirit. It is He who gives you the unction to function as a believer, whoever you are or whatever you represent.

He is the one Jesus talked about in ***John 16:7-16 (KJV)***

"Nevertheless I tell you the truth; It is expedient for you that I go away: for if I go not away, the <u>Comforter</u> will not come unto you; but if I depart, I will send him unto you. 8And when he is come, he will <u>reprove</u> the world of sin, and of

righteousness, and of judgment: 9Of sin, because they believe not on me; 10Of righteousness, because I go to my Father, and ye see me no more; 11Of judgment, because the prince of this world is judged. 12I have yet many things to say unto you, but ye cannot bear them now. 13Howbeit when he, the <u>Spirit of truth</u>, is come, he will <u>guide you into all truth</u>: for he shall not <u>speak</u> of himself; but whatsoever he shall hear, that shall he speak: and he will <u>shew you things to come</u>. 14He shall <u>glorify</u> me: for he shall receive of mine, and shall shew it unto you. 15All things that the Father hath are mine: therefore said I, that he shall take of mine, and shall shew it unto you. 16A little while, and ye shall not see me: and again, a little while, and ye shall see me, because I go to the Father."(Emphasis mine)

The Holy Spirit in a believer's life, according to Jesus, as quoted above, helps the believer (carrier) to do all the things underlined. His purposes are to comfort and counsel, correct and reprove man of sin, righteousness and judgment. He also guides and speaks the truth to us. He has come to reveal to us God the Father and the Son and their helpfulness to humanity; to display to us the power to do things seamlessly.

This unction from the Holy Spirit is strongly connected to passion. Passion is the key to excellence and success. Passion is the fire that drives everything including successful individuals, ministries, business organisations and more.

When you discover purpose, passion is what drives you to fulfil potential. Your seed, gift, talent is never enough without passion. In fact, a passionate person with limited gift will outperform a gifted person with little talent. This means that if you are not passionate as a leader or your organisation is not filled with people who are passionate about the vision, such organisation cannot achieve significance.

Therefore, if passion is connected to the Holy Spirit and everybody needs passion to drive success, then it means everybody needs the Holy Spirit.

Again, He is the One Jesus breathed on the disciples after His resurrection. *"Then said Jesus to them again, Peace be unto you: as my Father hath sent me, even so send I you. And when he had said this, he <u>breathed</u> on them, and saith unto them, <u>Receive</u> ye the Holy Ghost." John 20:21-22 (KJV) (emphasis mine).*

Notice that this is one of the few instances the word "breath" was used in the Bible. The first occurred in **Genesis 2:7**, when God originally created man out of dust. The prefix "re" in front of a word usually means again, so when Jesus said receive the Holy Ghost, he was referring to restoring Divine power to mankind again. This is how important He is to this generation.

> God will allow His anointing on you for a purpose.

The truth is, if the Holy Spirit is not working in your life, then you do not have the anointing. You must be at the point where your human spirit is overshadowed by God's Holy Spirit to possess this super ability to subdue, physically or spiritually, every force that is against your life, family and business.

The difference between this chapter and all the preceding ones is the statement above. God has created man with the ability to think, make own choices, have dominion, change things around us and focus on a goal and more. Every man has the capacity to do these naturally, even without the direct help of God in a sense. However,

He has given us His Holy Spirit to do more than what our human ability and knowledge put together can.

There is no limit to what you as a man can achieve and become when you live and work with the Holy Spirit. Everyone was created for an assignment. It is in your assignment you discover your purpose and in your purpose, you fulfil destiny. If men and women today are to effectively fulfil God's purpose for their lives, then they must constantly be filled with God's presence, power and passion, which only come through the fire of the Holy Spirit.

There cannot be passion without commitment. The Holy Spirit is the source of true commitment. Commitment means passion, energy, and intense enthusiasm. It comes from two Greek words meaning *'God theos'* infused and *'en'* God indwelt.

At this level of your life, business, career, ministry and more, you must demonstrate high level commitment in two key areas. The first is to your assignment and the second is to the people around you. It may be your employees or church workers and more.

First, you need a high level of commitment to your assignment because;

1. There are no great successes without obstacles or challenges.
2. Without commitment, you will never dig deep to develop all that is inbuilt in you that will lead you to greatness.
3. There are no great successes without great risk.
4. Without it you will be tempted to settle for the basis or minimum.

Secondly, you must show commitment to the people around you because;

1. People are committed to those who care for them.

2. People are committed to those they can trust.
3. People are committed to those who listen.
4. People are committed to those who know what they are doing.

To do all these rightly, you must seek to be connected to the Holy Spirit.

❖

The Purpose of the Anointing.

The anointing is for winning. It is for living a purpose-achieving life. If you desire to do more, then that is what you need. This is not for a select few; the Holy Spirit and His ability are for everyone who chooses to live in the body of Christ. To fulfil the fourth quadrant involves doing more than expected; asking more of yourself and giving more than others give and this requires special strength.

God will allow His anointing on you for a purpose. Every believer has a level of the anointing to operate from. All we need to do is to discover the purpose of God for our lives. As we do this, we discover the anointing. Jesus is our perfect example of this.

"The Spirit of the Lord is upon me, because he hath anointed me to preach the gospel to the poor; he hath sent me to heal the brokenhearted, to preach deliverance to the captives, and recovering of sight to the blind, to set at liberty them that are bruised," Luke 4:18 (KJV)

"How God anointed Jesus of Nazareth with the Holy Ghost and with power: who went about doing good, and healing

all that were oppressed of the devil; for God was with him."
Acts 10:38 (KJV)

This special ability was on Jesus for a special purpose; to heal, preach and set captives free, and in His life time He did just that. Beloved, the Holy Spirit needs you to manifest God's purpose through you. He dwells within you. Smith Wigglesworth said *"the unction of the Holy One is the Holy Spirit manifested in us. So we see that straight away within us there is the power to make manifest and bring forth those gifts which He has promised and these gifts will be manifested in proportion as we live in the unction of the Spirit of God.*

> He has given us His Holy Spirit to do more than what our human ability and knowledge put together can.

The Key to the Anointing

Who does not want to be successful in life or do things effortlessly? We all want to, and even those who believe there is no God will wish to receive this ability. But unlike any other abilities you have read in this book, there are conditions to receiving God's Holy Spirit.

1. **Obedience**

Obedience is yielding totally to God. This is the one thing God needs from you, for it is only those who are willing and obedient that shall receive this super power. Joshua is one man who demonstrated the power of God in great measure and right from the beginning of his leadership. All that God wanted from him was total obedience.

> All that God has is ours only when we yield and obey.

"Be strong and very courageous. Obey all the laws Moses gave you. Do not turn away from them, and you will be successful in everything you do". **Joshua 1:7 (NLT)**

Strength, courage and a focus concentration are all qualities you need as an individual and a leader to be successful in what you do. This is exactly what the Holy Spirit also brings to your life and leadership. If men and women can follow God's instructions, then His ability will freely but mightily flow through us.

God further warned Joshua to do three important things to demonstrate his obedience and submission to Him and these three things are what will still qualify you for the anointing.

"This book of the law shall not depart out of thy <u>mouth</u>; but thou shalt <u>meditate</u> therein day and night, that thou mayest observe to <u>do</u> according to all that is written therein: for then thou shalt make thy way prosperous, and then thou shalt have good success. **Joshua 1:8 (KJV) (emphasis mine).**

All that God demands from you to demonstrate your yieldedness to Him is to first speak His Word (mouth) and, secondly, think about His Word daily (meditate) and, thirdly, do what He says we should do; then good success and prosperity shall become our portion.

Obedience is basic because you have the power to do otherwise. Remember one of the abilities this book focuses on is that of choice. Like all other endowed abilities of man, we can work better when we partner what we have with God's. The result is having a fantastic advantage over the rest. Your abilities work better when you yield and surrender to God. You can be the best leader, business man, writer, author- you just name it—when you allow His anointing to come upon you.

If only God can have His way today; if only you can get rid of any hindrance in your human spirit , the Holy Spirit's anointing will come upon and smell on you to do mighty things. In **Acts 9:6,** Apostle Paul yielded when he cried out, *"what will thou have me do"* immediately he entered the call of God and that qualified him for this ability. It does not matter who you are. Paul was the worst of sinners, bringing many good men to prison, but when he yielded and obeyed, God granted him the unction to function. The truth is, all that God has is ours only when we yield and obey.

2. The Act of Righteousness

One of the fundamental issues related to the anointing is righteousness. This is simply loving and doing the right things in the sight of God because nothing pleases God more than living a holy life. There is something about holiness that graduates you into the anointing. Righteous living has the anointing in its illumination.

There seems to be a short supply of this ability today in our generation because we live in a moment where people love wickedness (sin) and hate righteousness. Doing the wrong things today is perceived by many to be the right things while we frown at righteous living. Whereas things are changing in the physical, the spiritual is different. Holiness is still vital in the kingdom of God; He is still holy as from the beginning. *"God is a Spirit and they that worship Him must do so in Spirit and in truth"*. **John 4:24 (KJV)**

This is why the level of your righteousness determines the level of anointing you carry. Purity is equal to power. There is a reciprocity nature of God where our level of faithfulness, integrity, humility and purity determines His towards us. Sin cripples us and places a limitation on the anointing. The reason why Jesus' anointing knew no limit was because He loved righteousness and knew no sin.

> If men and women can follow God's instructions, then His ability will freely but mightily flow through us.

"For he hath made him to be sin for us, who knew no sin; that we might be made the righteousness of God in him". **2 Corinthians 5:21 (KJV)**

In the same way in your life, this ever-increasing ability will know no limit when you pursue righteousness that knows no bound. *"You love what is right and hate what is wrong. Therefore God, your God, has anointed you, pouring out the oil of joy on you more than on anyone else."* **Psalm 45:7 (NLT)**

What a powerful verse! This means the more I love righteousness and hate evil or what is wrong, the more His anointing increases in and on me. I therefore determine the level of this ability by my own doing and nothing else.

3. The Act of Thirsting, Hungering and Panting

Another problem with us today is we are not thirsty and hungry for the ability in the spirit. We

> The level of your righteousness determines the level of anointing you carry.

rather thirst and hunger for physical things such as food and water and what money can buy. God wants you to thirst and hunger for Him because it is only those who pant, thirst and hunger for Him that go for the anointing.

"As the deer pants for streams of water, so I long for you, O God. 2I thirst for God, the living God. When can I come and stand before him? **Psalm 42:1-2 (NLT)**

"A Psalm of David, when he was in the wilderness of Judah. O God, thou art my God; early will I seek thee: my soul thirsteth for thee, my flesh longeth for thee in a dry and thirsty land, where no water is" **Psalm 63:1 (KJV)**

"Is anyone thirsty? Come and drink—even if you have no money! Come, take your choice of wine or milk—it's all free! 2Why spend your money on food that does not give you strength? Why pay for food that does you no good? Listen, and I will tell you where to get food that is good for the soul. **Isaiah 55:1-2 (NLT)**

These scriptures certainly demonstrate to you that there is something more than physical food and water and that you should not only spend time thinking and worrying about what to eat and wear. The soul without the thirst and hunger for the Word of God is on its way to death. After all, the only man that is not thirsty is a dead man. This anointing is for only those who will thirst and hunger for more of God.

The Vitality of the Anointing

Everyone, especially a child of God, needs the anointing. You cannot achieve quadrant four (subduing) without walking in the anointing/passion. Remember the underlying analysis in this book; God has endowed you with the ability to be fruitful, multiply and replenish. However, to overcome challenges, limitations and problems at the top of your life, career, business or even ministry requires special abilities and strength and this is where the Holy Spirit's anointing/passion is vital.

We are living in accelerated times. Everything is moving fast, and as a result, we need the anointing for key reasons, if we are to overcome challenges and complex problems in everything we do.

The question still remains why this ability if I possess all other abilities. You will discover, among other things, that the anointing is vital in very key areas after you have been fruitful, multiplied and even replenished.

I. You need the anointing for effective living

An effective living is one that is results-oriented. This is the only ability that will bring fulfilment to your life because nothing gets accomplished without the anointing.

II. The anointing brings restoration

When the anointing is operating in a man's life, there is an act of renewal and reestablishment. Things lost in your life, family, career, and even business can be located and restored. This is because the anointing is a symbol of the presence and power of the Holy Spirit of God in your life.

If you study the life of King Saul from **1Samuel 10:1-16,** you will discover among several truths that operating in the anointing brings restoration. In v1, immediately the oil (symbol of the anointing) fell on the head of Saul, things that were lost were straightaway found. His family's donkeys (business) that had strayed away for days were found as Samuel anointed Saul.

Before this ability fell on Saul's head, remember he had been searching for the same donkeys for days to no avail. It is not until he was empowered with this ability that things were restored. May be you too are at a point where your life, family, marriage, business, etc. need a next level idea, plan or solution to achieve complete dominion or reign.

III. The anointing ushers you in to supernatural progress

This is simply divine favour. The Grace of God comes upon everyone who walks and lives in the anointing. God's favour works for us and grants us things we have not worked or bargained for. Supernatural progress also means that your life, business, ministry, etc. begin to move forward. Again, I want you to stay focused on the life of Saul. After his encounter with Samuel, his life began to move in supernatural dimensions.

1 Samuel 10:3-4 (NLT) continues, *"When you get to the oak of Tabor, you will see three men coming toward you who are on their way to worship God at Bethel. One will be bringing three young goats, another will have three loaves of bread, and the third will be carrying a skin of wine. 4They will greet you and offer you two of the loaves, which you are to accept.*

The anointing over a carrier's life propels him to move forward just as we see in the case of Saul. The three items mentioned *(bread, young goat and wine)* represent supernatural abundance. You may be like Saul who was from the lowest and weakest tribe, but when you walk in this ability, there is no limit to what you can become.

Bread is a symbol for new life in Christ and sustaining truth. This is why **John 6:35** *says "And Jesus said unto them, I am the bread of life: he that cometh to me shall never hunger; and he that believeth on me shall never thirst."* Bread is also a symbol of revelation gift.

The *wine* is also a symbol for doctrine, which represents a new level of ideas and understanding, and a new covenant. When you embrace this passion, you embrace the new, as old things give way. **Luke 5:37** reads, *"And no one puts new wine into old wineskins. The new wine would burst the old skins, spilling the wine and ruining the skins."* Wine also is a symbol of spiritual value.

Goat in the Bible has different meanings. However, goats in the Old Testament and in this case represent fertility, vitality and ceaseless energy.

IV. The anointing also grants you power for supernatural change

This will cause people to wonder about the sudden change. The kind of accelerated change that goes beyond man's ability to produce. In the case study above, the young man Saul's life and the family business experienced an exponential change when he encountered the anointing.

- ❖ **Are you at a point when you desire supernatural change?**
- ❖ **Have you been fruitful, multiplied and replenished but yet lack the catalyst to achieve dominion?**

Then seek no further, thirst and yearn for the anointing.

V. You need the anointing to deal with the devil

We are living in an age where one cannot underestimate the power, schemes and plans of the devil. The Bible makes it clear that Satan's agenda is to steal, kill and destroy your life, faith, career, marriage, business, etc. and even to deny you of personal growth. Do not be deceived by the rapid and continuous emergence of technological advancement the world is experiencing today. Satan is and still remains the god of this age (2 Corinthians 4:4) and the ruler of the kingdom of this world.

The key to deal with Satan and his schemes is through faith and the anointing. It does not matter who you are, whether you believe or not, the fact still remains that spiritual things control physical things. This is why in God's ordinance; the fourth quadrant requires deeper spiritual insights to succeed. At this level in business or personal life, hard work is a requirement, but hard work without the anointing is not enough. So stay alert and stand firm in faith and the anointing–**1 Peter 5:8-9 (NLT)**.

VI. **You need the anointing to break curses** If something is not a blessing, usually it is a curse. A curse is something that brings or causes great trouble or harm to you, family, marriage, career and even more. It is also an appeal or prayer for evil or misfortune to befall someone or something. Can it be possible that the reason why your business cannot experience a major breakthrough is as a result of a curse or even your life, marriage, career and more? If yes, there are three (3) levels of curses this book brings to your attention.

   1. **Ancestral Curses:** These are curses handed down from your great great grandfathers or ancestors you never met. The truth is just as you can walk into a blessing you never laboured for, so can you walk under a curse you know

nothing about. This is how dangerous curses are. Until something is done about them, curses from those of old can destroy lives, families, marriages and everything you can think of.

2. **Generational Curses:** These are curses handed down from family members you know. It can be your parents or even siblings. This is why under the chapter on choices, it has been clearly started that most times, the choices we make have consequences not only for us but also for our generation. Can it be that the family business for years could not subdue the terrains because of this or have you observed a current trend in your family line?

3. **Personal Curses:** These are curses inflicted upon you either by the devil, someone or even your own doing. As long as a curse is standing, no amount of hard work, career enhancement, educational pedigree, leadership development alone is enough to grant you the highest dominion. You may be fruitful and sometimes attain fruit multiplication, but to replenish, and especially subdue, you need something higher and stronger than such curses. This is what the Holy Spirit's ability offers you and this is one reason why you and I need the anointing, the most important influence on earth.

VII. You need the anointing to change your seasons

A season is a flexible space of time usually in the spiritual realm which carries and unleashes deep

> Competence will always get you very far, but character always determines how long you will handle promotions as they come your way.

revelation truths. Season controls everything, including time and purpose. *"To everything there is a season, a time to every purpose under the earth."* **Ecclesiastes 3:1 (NLT)**. Just as there are seed time and harvest time, so there are deep spiritual and even physical seasons characterised by revelations and change that require understanding in order to seize kairos moments.

Missing seasons therefore can create catastrophic effects in a person's life and business. The key to understanding and taking opportunities of seasons to walk in kingdom dominion is through the Holy Spirit Who reveals the mind of God.

"And he changeth the times and the seasons: he removeth kings, and setteth up kings: he giveth wisdom unto the wise, and knowledge to them that know understanding." **Daniel 2:21 (KJV)**.

This also means that through the Holy Spirit, seasons can be changed to favour you if need be.

VIII. **You need the anointing to overcome limitations**

A limitation is a boundary, a restriction or final point drawn by man or obstacles in life. One key purpose of this book is to reveal to you the structural levels of your dominion mandate using the four principles of fruitfulness, multiplication, replenishment and subdue.

It is very realistic for one to be fruitful and never go beyond the rest of the quadrants / principles.

Though persistence, consistency, tenacity, hard work and keys to leadership and personal or corporate growth are contributing factors and necessary tools in becoming better and productive in your endeavours, this book adds that spiritual aspects of life should never be undermined. This is why the power of faith and the Holy Spirit are being emphasised at this level of the quadrants.

IX. You need the anointing to work

Your work is your assignment in life and every assignment is connected to destiny. Destiny is the source of purpose and in your purpose you discover your calling. This is why for you to fully discover yourself, it begins with understanding what you have been called (born) to be, which leads to your purpose and destiny in life, before understanding your assignment which becomes your work on earth.

Hence work is what you do to benefit others (i.e., other than yourself). To effectively carry your work on earth, the anointing acts as a divine enabler to help you impact fully your generation.

X. You need the anointing to handle promotions at your next level

This is what the fourth quadrant of subduing is all about. It is about reaching the next level and be sustained in dimensions. Many people and even companies work hard to reach greater heights but few develop the capacity to handle promotions at this level. Competence will always get you very far, but character always determines how long you will handle promotions as they come your way.

Competence can be built by your certificates and technical abilities, but true character and integrity are built by deep spiritual qualities which the Holy Spirit offers in abundance.

Finally, do you know this Person? Do you have a relationship with the Holy Spirit? The grace and love of God are free but the Holy Ghost requires fellowship to operate in you effectively. Fellowship simply means a friendly association with a person(s) sharing similar interests, ideals, or experiences on equal terms. This means that, for you to triumph and taste victory, the Holy Spirit requires your effort together with His power.

These are what it takes to subdue in quadrant four. I do not think anything is higher than what you have just read.

APPLYING THE POWER OF THE HOLY SPIRIT QUADRANT FOUR (SUBDUE)

1. To fulfil the fourth quadrant involves doing more than expected; asking more of yourself and giving more than others give and this requires special strength.
2. Persistence, consistency, tenacity, hard work and keys to leadership and personal or corporate growth are contributing factors and necessary tools in becoming better and productive in your endeavours, however, on top of all of these is the Holy Ghost power because of what He brings.
3. The anointing is a divine enabler that comes from God the Holy Ghost. Gaining this power is simply inheriting God's 'super' on your 'natural' or His 'extra' on your 'ordinary' to do the supernatural and the extraordinary.
4. If passion is connected to the Holy Spirit and everybody needs passion to drive success, then it means everybody needs the Holy Spirit.
5. The anointing is vital in very key areas after you have been fruitful, multiplied and even replenished. You need the anointing ;
   I. For effective living.
   II. To brings restoration.
   III. To ushers you in to supernatural progress
   IV. To deal with the devil
   V. To break curses.
   VI. To change your seasons.
   VII. To overcome limitations.
   VIII. To work
   IX. To handle promotions at your next level

6. At this level of quadrant four as a person, leader, businessman, pastor, it is about legacy building. You have been fruitful, multiplied and even replenished but to build a lasting legacy through people, you need special strength and this is what the Holy Spirit's passion comes to offer.
7. Always remember that success (fruitful, multiply) without a successor (replenish, subdue) is failure. Don't fail when the Holy Spirit can help. Add Him to your life, team, organisation and build a lasting legacy.

QUADRANT FOUR (SUBDUE)

THE POWER OF LOVE (RENEWAL)

'The chain that hooks and connects these four (4) magnificent quadrants together.'

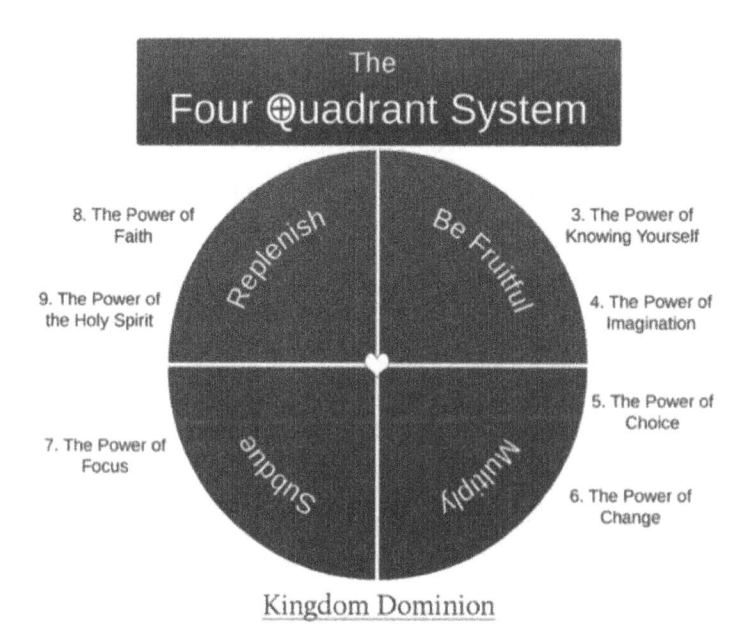

The Four Quadrant System

- 8. The Power of Faith
- 9. The Power of the Holy Spirit
- 7. The Power of Focus
- 3. The Power of Knowing Yourself
- 4. The Power of Imagination
- 5. The Power of Choice
- 6. The Power of Change

Quadrants: Replenish, Be Fruitful, Subdue, Multiply

Kingdom Dominion

10

THE POWER OF LOVE

This chapter is unique and special because it embodies all the four dimensional principles of God's dominion mandate to man, which are that every man was created to be *fruitful, to multiply, to replenish and to subdue*, according to **Genesis 1:26-28.** It also serves as the foundation to everything discussed in this book. This is why it forms the last chapter of this manifesto. The power of God's love to mankind surrounds everything because it is the ability that makes even the impossible possible.

Before you continue, permit me to shed light on what you have read up till this level. So far in this book, you have discovered what I refer to us the four quadrants to success. These four quadrants are precisely from the first statement of the Creator(God), when He said after creating man (male and female); be **fruitful, multiply, replenish** and **subdue** according to Genesis 1:26-28.

This has been the premises of this book. The first requirement of greatness is to become *fruitful* with what you have. The word fruitful simply means productivity, yielding results. To do this, you have to identify your seed; which is your gift, talent, and what you carry. The reason why God never said be seedful but fruitful is because every living thing on the surface of this earth has a seed, already planted in him/her from birth. The ability to know yourself and imagine are key requiments to fulfil this important quadrant of greatness.

The second requirement to greatness is your ability to *multiply* your fruits. The quadrant multiply simply refers to increase. In order words, in the eyes of the Manufacturer of man, it is not enough to yield results, you have got to increase what you have. This is why the power of choice and change has been treated in this book, to help you move from fruit bearing to fruit multiplication as an individual, leader or whoever you are.

> The key to understanding your mandate to rule and control is, first and foremost, learning to love.

After multiplying your fruits, you still have to move forward to the third quadrant; which is *replenish*. In the cover of this book have you discovered the neccessity to continue and be consistant with what you have produced as an author, artist, student, pastor or even a business owner. You need a focused concentration at this level of the quadrants to remain relevant to your generation.

To achieve what I call dominion mandate, which is the epitome of greatness, you must press on to the final quadrant, which is *subdue*. It takes high level of character, commitment and capacity beyond just skills and qualifications to ensure that you live a positive legacy for generations. This is why this book has introduced you to the passion of the Holy Ghost and more.

The purpose of this chapter therefore is to teach you that, although each quadrant can be pursued independently, it is not until they are fulfilled interdependently that one can really walk in full dominion. If the four quadrants are habits that must be followed, the love principle is the chain that hooks and connects these four (4) magnificent quadrants together.

If true and genuine love is not at the centre of your heart then you may not succeed to be fruitful or even multiply your efforts, so to achieve complete dominion, unconditional love must be at the centre of your life, family, career, business and even ministry. When unconditional love is at the centre of what you do, even all the four dimensions of your nature – physical, spiritual, mental and social/emotional–will manifest God's glory.

This is why the simple principle of 'love what you do' and 'do what you love' is key in walking in Kingdom dominion because if you do not love what you are doing, how then can you go beyond quadrant 1, which is fruitfulness? For instance, a man may be a very successful business man and even make lots of money, but if he has no love for his customers, how far will such a person go? You may be a professional in anything in this world, but if your service is mere profession with no love for what you do, then you cannot leave any great legacy behind.

If you do not have love for God and man, you are like what the Bible says, a sounding brass and tinkling cymbal. This unconditional love must be shed abroad in your heart, whether you are a businessman, family man, student or even a seller at the market. The question therefore is, *how can one achieve this*?

When your love for God is strong, it will affect your love for mankind and this will affect everything you seek to achieve such as career, ministry, or family. This kind of love produces results that go beyond **storge** (*affection*), **phillia** (*friendship*), or **eros** (*romance*). This is not to underestimate such kinds of love, but it is the agape or unconditional kind of love that has profound affection on others,

The Power of Love

compelling one to serve another. This love is greater than human love or man's love towards the Father. It is one you can depend on because it comes directly from God and He cannot change neither can He fail.

The secret to fulfilling our dominion mandate is that, at each quadrant, there are challenges to overcome, especially in quadrant four (to subdue), where you must conquer and overcome obstacles against you if you want to succeed and leave a lasting, positive legacy. When you encounter a man who understands and constantly feeds on the love of God towards him, you discover one who cannot be defeated, no matter the level of dificulty or challenge. Why, you may ask? Because if the Lord of Lords (owner of all owners) loves you, who can be against you.

> The key to knowing that God loves and is for you but never against you comes from the simple fact that He did not spare His Son

*"[32] He that spared not his own Son, but delivered him up for us all, how shall he not with him also freely give us all things? [33] Who shall lay anything to the charge of God's elect? It is God that justifieth.[34] Who is he that condemneth? It is Christ that died, yea rather, that is risen again, who is even at the right hand of God, who also maketh intercession for us.[35] Who shall separate us from the love of Christ? Shall **tribulation**, or **distress**, or **persecution**, or **famine**, or **nakedness**, or **peril**, or **sword**?[38]For I am persuaded, that neither **death**, nor **life**, nor **angels**, nor **principalities**, nor **powers**, nor things **present**, nor things to come,[39]Nor **height**, nor **depth**, nor any other **creature**, shall be able to separate us from the love of God, which is in Christ Jesus our Lord"* Romans 8:32-35 (emphasis mine).

The key to knowing that God loves and is for you but never against you comes from the simple fact that He did not spare His Son from dying for you and He is interceding for you. Now I have put in bold in the text above over seventeen (17) things that cannot defeat a man who knows and understands the love of God for him or her. Meditate on such now.

Notice also that these more than seventeen things are exactly what the quadrants, especially quadrant four (to subdue), require you to thrive against. Again, I must emphasise that these principles are for everyone, not just for a chosen few. It affects every facet of life. Any man who will feed on God's love for him will be set free from every obstacle.

> *For you were called to freedom, brothers. Only do not use your freedom as an opportunity for the flesh, but through* **love** *serve one another.* **Galatians 5:13 (NLT)**

> *"For God so loved the world, that he gave his only begotten Son, that whosoever believeth in him should not perish, but have everlasting life.* **John 3:16 (KJV)**

Today, the world is broken and powerless, complete dominion mandate is scarcely realistic because such love is being lost. Economies, businesses and families are collapsing because the God kind of love is ceasing to exist. The number one plan of the enemy is targeted at causing people to believe that there is no God and that He does not love us. When the enemy succeeds in this way, it limits or even cuts short God's ability being imparted to us because it is only through our confidence that God's might is released.

Men who built lasting legacy (Quadrant Four)

The case of Biblical character **Job** is a perfect example. This man was fruitful in every sense. He had been fruitful and even multiplied his fruits as a family man, businessman and all you can think of. However, the devil, our greatest adversary, launched a brutal attack on his life and whatever he represented.

"[13] One day when Job's sons and daughters were feasting at the oldest brother's house, [14] a messenger arrived at Job's home with this news: "Your oxen were plowing, with the donkeys feeding beside them, [15] when the Sabeans raided us. They stole all the animals and killed all the farmhands. I am the only one who escaped to tell you.[16] While he was still speaking, another messenger arrived with this news: "The fire of God has fallen from heaven and burned up your sheep and all the shepherds. I am the only one who escaped to tell you."[17]

While he was still speaking, a third messenger arrived with this news: "Three bands of Chaldean raiders have stolen your camels and killed your servants. I am the only one who escaped to tell you."[18] While he was still speaking, another messenger arrived with this news: "Your sons and daughters were feasting in their oldest brother's home. [19] Suddenly, a powerful wind swept in from the wilderness and hit the house on all sides. The house collapsed, and all your children are dead. I am the only one who escaped to tell you."[20] Job stood

> Love and sound mind possess equal authority.

up and tore his robe in grief. Then he shaved his head and fell to the ground to worship." Job 1:13-20

In just a day, all his businesses (donkey, sheep, and camel), workers and family were attacked and destroyed. Can you imagine this happening to anybody? No, not even to your worst enemy. This was too bad that even his wife at a point instigated him to curse God, something we all can do in such situations, but Job knew the love of God for his life and so did not do it. *How well do you know this love?*

⁹His wife said to him, "Are you still trying to maintain your integrity? Curse God and die."¹⁰But Job replied, "You talk like a foolish woman. Should we accept only good things from the hand of God and never anything bad?" So in all this, Job said nothing wrong.

Job's life is teaching us a fundamental principle in walking and achieving complete dominion. This is that under no condition should one doubt the love of God for one. As he believed even at the point of losing everything he had ever worked for, so we must also believe that God's love for us is unconditional, unfailing and unending.

The fear of losing everything did not stop him (Job) from loving God. One of the things that will stop you from achieving your dominion mandate is FEAR; *False Evidence Appearing Real.* If you are to win at every level of the quadrant, you must deal with fear. The fear of the unknown, fear of what people may say or not say, fear of failure and more are some of the reasons why many never fulfil dominion or even fall from grace to grass.

═══════════════════════════════
Economies, businesses and families are collapsing because the God kind of love is ceasing to exist.
═══════════════════════════════

The opposite of love is not only hatred but also fear, a key tool of Satan to stop us from achieving complete dominion. God on the other

The Power of Love

hand gives us three (3) things to walk in dominion. They are *Power*, *Love*, and *Sound Mind*, the three key empowerment of the Holy Spirit.

> *"7For God has not given us a spirit of fear, but of power and of love and of a sound mind." (*2 Timothy 1:7) (NLT)

It is not a mistake that in between power and sound mind is the love of God. The love of God therefore must take centre stage in one's life in order to achieve complete dominion. Many a times, people are tempted to go for the power of the Holy Spirit, but love and sound mind possess equal authority. No wonder the end of Job's life clearly defines for us what it means to walk in dominion. The Bible records in Job 42:10-16 the latter end of this man's life.

> *"10 And the Lord restored Job's losses[a] when he prayed for his friends. Indeed the Lord gave Job twice as much as he had before. 11 Then all his brothers, all his sisters, and all those who had been his acquaintances before, came to him and ate food with him in his house; and they consoled him and comforted him for all the adversity that the Lord had brought upon him. Each one gave him a piece of silver and each a ring of gold.*
>
> *12 Now the Lord blessed the latter days of Job more than his beginning; for he had fourteen thousand sheep, six thousand camels, one thousand yoke of oxen, and one thousand female donkeys. 13 He also had seven sons and three daughters. 14 And he called the name of the first Jemimah, the name of the*

> You cannot kill the beloved of God.

second Keziah, and the name of the third Keren-Happuch.
¹⁵ In all the land were found no women so beautiful as the daughters of Job; and their father gave them an inheritance among their brothers.

¹⁶ After this Job lived one hundred and forty years, and saw his children and grandchildren for four generations. ¹⁷ So Job died, old and full of days."

This is what happens to the man who walks in God's love for mankind. I claim this for you in Jesus' name. Amen.

Joseph: A young man who also knew and understood the love of God is the Biblical character Joseph. This man represents in our generation a man who talks and walks in the love of God for him. All that Joseph communicated to his family was how God loved him and, as a result, his dream was going to manifest. No wonder this man can be described as one of the few men who walked in total dominion. He fulfilled the four quadrants; he was fruitful, he multiplied, he replenished and he subdued.

His brothers on the other hand represent in our generation people who feed their mind on hatred and fear. Today people can be passionately filled with fear and hate that it stops them from walking in their dominion mandate. This magnificent power of love cannot operate where there is fear or hate. This explains why Joseph's brothers had to get rid of him from amongst them. In the same way, the enemy can paralyse you with fear and disable you from walking in dominion.

In the life of **Joseph** also do we discover the price of love – PAIN. It was because of love that he had to go through all that he went through. Not only was it painful for his brothers to hate him with passion, they had plans to kill him, which later changed because you cannot kill the beloved of God. They instead put him in a **PIT** "*Prime minister In Training*" and sold their own flesh and blood into slavery in a foreign land. He became a slave in Potiphar's house, was lied against by Potiphar's wife, thrown into prison, forgotten by many and more. This is pain.

In his book, *The Portrait of Love*, **Eastwood Anaba** stated and I quote: *"love travels in the veins of pain. Agape love can only be transported in the medium of pain. You have to learn to thank God for your pains because without it, you will be loveless."*

> The love of God looks at what will come out of you at the end (product) and not what you will go through (process).

In the same light, the price to pay for the love of your family, business, ministry, etc. is usually through the pain you go through to sustain them. You may be going through a season in your life right now that is making you to ask the question: "IF GOD WANTS US TO ACHIEVE DOMINION, WHY ALL THESE OBSTACLES, CHALLENGES AND PAINS?"

Jesus Christ: It is not wrong to ask this question because Jesus, even as the beloved of God, went through so much pain to the point that not only did he ask God to *let this cup pass by Him* at one point, he even cried out *"Lord, why have you forsaken me?"* We cannot deny the truth that God loved and was pleased with Jesus, even while here on earth (Matthew 17:5).

However, the bible says in **Isaiah 53:10** that, *yet it* **pleased** *the Lord to* **bruise him***; he hath put him to* **grief***: when thou shalt make his soul an offering for sin, he shall see his seed, he shall prolong his days, and* **the pleasure of the Lord** *shall prosper in his hand."*

We are still answering your question using the lives of Jesus and Joseph as case studies. The verse above says that it was the pleasure of the Lord towards Jesus that bruised him and caused him grief. The word "pleasure" in Isaiah 53:10 means the Lord's purpose or plan. So God's purpose towards Jesus caused Him pain for the prosperity of the world in his hand.

Now to answer the above question directly, the power of His dominion mandate to us also means that God will allow those He loves to go through pain, if it will lead to the fulfilment of His ultimate purpose for their lives. This magnificent power of God's love deals with us in a way that focuses on the product of our pain and not the process of it. The love of God looks at what will come out of you at the end (product) and not what you will go through (process).

> The price of love is PAIN.

So the fact that you are going through what you are going through currently does not mean that you are a sinner or bad person and as a result God's love is not for you. On the other hand, the fact that God loves you does not also mean that you will live a problem- or pain-free life. This is why the fourth quadrant requires you to subdue, which means to learn to overcome challenges, problems and pain to your breakthrough.

This is also not to forget men whose legacies are there today for us to follow. Men like Nelson Mandela, Victor Franklyn, Steve Job and more, whose stories run through this book, and who have passed through higher levels of pain but never allowed such to break them. They understood quadrant four and developed the habit of placing unconditional love above them and as such achieved dominion. Today we celebrate their legacy.

These men are role models for today's generation. As you have seen, no matter what they went through, they still understood that God loved them and that understanding lifted each one of them to a greater height. My Bible says the Pharisees could not withstand Jesus when they found out that they could not stop Him, Pilate could not find any fault in Him, Herod could not kill Him and even death could not hold Him, all because of the power of God's love towards Him.

What is LOVE?

Now let us attempt to define LOVE, especially in the context of God's dominion mandate to mankind.

1. *Love is God's unconditional ability and power over your life, which helps you to achieve complete dominion.*
2. *Love is the capacity to hold on and overcome in the midst of pressure, persecution and pain, with the full assurance that God is for and not against me.*
3. *Love is also the cord that binds us to the bosom of the Father.*
4. *Love is living in the fearless understanding that God is for you and never against you, no matter what comes your way in life.*
5. *Love is the demonstration of the exact presence of God with a force immeasurable and incomprehensible.*
6. *It is the most effective physical, spiritual, social and even emotional weapon on earth, which leads to liberation of those in captivity and bondage.*
7. *Love is that which can cause a man to be tried and tested temporarily but never to be denied and destroyed permanently.*
8. *This love is that which permits God to focus on the product of our destiny and not the process of our lives. This does not mean that God is not interested in the process of your life; He*

> *is still concerned with and supervises the process as a means to an end.*

Above all, **1 Corinthians 13** offers you the best definition of this magnificent power of love. I entreat you to study this text in detail, as due to space constraint we cannot delve into it in this book.

> *"Love is **patient** and **kind**. Love is **not jealous** or **boastful** or **proud** [5] or **rude**. It does not demand its own way. It is **not irritable**, and it keeps no record of **being wronged**. [6] It does **not rejoice** about injustice but **rejoices whenever the truth wins out**. [7] Love **never gives up**, **never loses faith**, is always **hopeful,** and endures through every circumstance. [13] Three things will last forever—faith, hope, and love—and the greatest of these is love."* **1 Corinthians 13:4-7, 13** (emphasis mine).

To thrust further, notice that this portion of God's word is revealing to you a powerful secret to fulfilling the quadrants no matter the circumstances and challenges that will arise.

Here in lies the secret; when a man/woman loves what he does and does what he loves unconditionally, he/she is patient, kind not jealous or boastful. He let go of others wrongs to get hold of what lies ahead. He celebrates other people's successes and victories. Because of love, he does not give up or lose confidence irrespective of the circumstance for the reason that, genuine love never fails.

Living and walking in unconditional love

Now that you know about His love as a powerful weapon to fulfil your dominion mandate, the question we will answer is "WHAT DO

YOU DO TO APPROPRIATE THE LOVE OF GOD FOR EVERY ASPECT OF YOUR DESTINY?"

1. Meditate on His love for you every day of your life

There is power of meditation. The word "meditate" simply means to ponder on something over and over again until it becomes part of you. Purposefully know daily that God loves you and He is for you. God is never against you and all things are working together for your good.

"The Lord is on my side; I will not fear: what can man do unto me?" Psalm 118:7

Wake up daily and intentionally feed your mind with the truth that you are God's beloved. I particularly used the adverb *"intentionally"* because this is what growth is about. You must specifically intend to grow; if not, you will never grow in any area of your life, including in this wonderful love of God. As you feed your mind with this truth, you will discover how powerful the love of God is to every situation you are facing, especially in the areas of your dominion mandate.

2. Seek to be deeply rooted in this love

Let this become your vital desire in life. Prioritise your life, ministry, career, business and whatever concerns you around the love of God. Let it be the very prayer you pray.

"17 and I pray that Christ will make his home in your hearts as you trust in him. Your roots will grow down into God's love and keep you strong. 18 And may you have the power to understand, as all God's people should, how wide, how long, how high, and how deep his love

is. *[19] May you experience the love of Christ, though it is too great to understand fully. Then you will be made complete with all the fullness of life and power that comes from God.*

[20] Now all glory to God, who is able, through his mighty power at work within us, to accomplish infinitely more than we might ask or think. [21] Glory to him in the church and in Christ Jesus through all generations forever and ever! Amen." **Galatians 3:17-20 (NLT)**

Out of this powerful scripture come **<u>five (5) prayer points</u>** you can inculcate into your life, family, business and even ministry, concerning this love of God.

i. Prayer to keep you deeply rooted in God's love to receive supernatural strength to win.

ii. Pray for the power to understand His love as you should in its:
   - **Width**: *Covering every area of your experience.*
   - **Length**: *To continue all the days of your life.*
   - **Height**: *To lift you in victory and celebration.*
   - **Depth**: *To reach you even in your despair, discouragement, doubt, delay and even defeat.*

iii. Prayer to be filled with the fullness of this powerful love that comes from God.

iv. Prayer to activate this power to be at work in you to accomplish mighty things beyond your own level of expectations.

v. Pray and ask Him to do this in your life and take back all the glory.

3. Pursue a pure heart and a good conscience

Love springs up by itself from a pure heart and a good conscience. A heart that loves is only a heart that has been touched. It is only when your heart is touched by this unconditional love of God that you will be able to subdue every force against your life, ministry or business and build a lasting legacy.

4. Walk in this love

You are not supposed to only know this love. Walk in the practicality of it, whether in your life, home, business or more. There is a thin line between knowing and doing. A lot of people know the love of God but few people demonstrate this love in the face of adversity. 'Love' even as a word can be used as a verb, which simply connotes that love is a doing or an action word. Also, we walk in love by being love, because God is love.

> *"Imitate God, therefore, in everything you do, because you are his dear children. ² Live a life filled with love, following the example of Christ. He loved us[a] and offered himself as a sacrifice for us, a pleasing aroma to God."* **Ephesians 3:1-2**

> *"Dear children, let's not merely say that we love each other; let us show the truth by our actions.¹⁹ Our actions will show that we belong to the truth, so we will be confident when we stand before God"* **1John 3:18-19 (NLT)**

It is very clear from these verses that God expects us to go beyond learning and knowing about His love to living and walking fully in it, as in our actions alone lies the proof of the truth of our dominion mandate. As you have read in this chapter, true love is the embodiment of the creator's first commandment to mankind. Whether man will be fruitful, multiply, replenish and subdue begins with knowing and walking in His love.

APPLYING THE POWER OF LOVE QUADRANT FOUR (SUBDUE)

1. Unconditional love is key because it is the cord that binds all the four quadrants together. Begin by seeking the unconditional love of God in your heart and let it take centre stage in your life, business, ministry and more.
2. The basic principle of unconditional love is this: *do what you love and love what you do*. Apply this principle in everything you do, even as a professional. Money is good and a necessity today, but never let it be your number one priority. Instead, first love what you do and do what you love.
3. The opposite of love is not only hatred but fear. Fight every form of fear limiting your moving forward.
4. The price of love is pain. Let this quote empower you to move forward. *"Love travels in the veins of pain. Agape love can only be transported in the medium of pain. You have to learn to thank God for your pains because without it, you will be loveless."* **Eastwood Anaba**
5. Live and walk in unconditional love daily by:
   ❖ Meditating on God's love.
   ❖ Seeking through prayers to be deeply rooted in it.
   ❖ Walking in clear conscience.
6. Let the 5 prayer points shared in this book guide you daily as a counsellor, accountant, pastor and more.
7. Practically act in love in all your transactions; live a life filled with love, even for your enemies. Let the love of God be shed abroad in your heart.

8. Develop first a strong love for God, which secondly will affect your love for mankind, and this will finally reflect in every fibre of your being.

Finally, I hope this book has been a blessing to you and whatsoever you represent. However, do you have this unconditional love of God inside of you? If not, maybe you need to consider inviting God into your life. This is what you need to connect you to what God has purposed for you. If you agree with me, why don't you recite the following words in your heart and with your mouth?

"Lord Jesus, thank you for today, I have heard your word about love and Kingdom dominion. I welcome you into my heart; forgive me all my sins and come and live inside of me through your Holy Spirit. Thank you for making me new in Jesus' name. Amen."

If you just said this prayer, you are a new person from today. Find a Bible-believing church and begin to grow from there. God bless you.

ABOUT THE AUTHOR

Kofi Owusu Amoateng is a Power Speaker, Writer, Teacher and Ordained Minister of the Gospel. He is the founder of the Purpose Achieving Life Group, an organisation which empowers individuals and corporate organisations to discover Primary Purpose through Partnerships, Seminars, Consultancy, Article Publications and more.

He is also the founder of the AFAP Coaching School which is a Coaching, Mentoring and Leadership programme designed to train people to Discover, Dedicate and Develop their primary assignment. He is the author of the famous book Alive For A Purpose.

He is currently the Head Servant (Pastor) of Newjoy International Gospel Church, UK. He empowers and motivates thousands of individuals yearly through several Speaking Engagements, Seminars and Publications on various topics including Purpose, Potential, Passion, Leadership, Personal Development and more.

Kofi is married to Rhoda and together they have three wonderful kids, Christine, Ephraim and Immanuel.

Authors Contact
www.purposeachievinglife.com
www.nigc.org.uk
www.aliveforapurpose/facebook
pal@purposeachievinglife.com

ACKNOWLEDGEMENT

Books are idea containers and in them lay the capacity of changing lives. From the time it is conceived by the author to the moment it is felt and touched, so many people make meaningful contributions in order to make it possible.

I would like to thank…

Dr. Amos Fatokun PHD. You edited this book to perfection. Words are not enough to say thank you and for that, I am eternally grateful and also to your wonderful wife, Bukola Fatokun, my dear sister, for your valuable encouragement all the way through.

Pastor Ken Omeje PHD for being a mentor, father and an encourager throughout the years. You are an example of people God can use to lift others and I am very grateful to you.

Pastor Steve Asante (Asokwa Baptist Church, Ghana), daddy, for being so much of a blessing to me and family, I say thanks to you and the entire Asokwa church members.

Brother Joey and first lady Vinnette Hollingworth, you are such an inspiration to the Body of Christ. May the Lord continue to use you for mighty things.

Lydia J.J, it is such a joy to see how the very principles in this book keep changing your life from one level to another. I have mentored many people but you are unique and special. Keep moving forward.

The Purpose Achieving Life and AFAP Coaching School Team, especially Anuoluwapo for designing the Four Quadrant Dominion Mandate System.

Valuable friends and family, Mansford and Abigail, Kofi Atuahene and Martha, Sammy and Daniel Ninson, Peter and Cecilia. I thank God for your friendships.

To my mothers, Nana Afia Osa aka Mama Sister, Aunty Monica, my dear siblings Benita and Marlise, Cousins, Papa Yaw, Junior aka Dun D, I love you all.

To my in-laws, Mum Philomena, Nana Owusu Korkor, Patricia and the entire family, I am grateful.

To all Newjoy International Gospel Church family, you guys rock. You are my real family.

Finally, to everyone who has contributed one way or the other to my life and purpose, I thank you in the name of our Lord Jesus Christ. I hope that this book remains a blessing until eternity, amen.

NOTES

Jim C. (2001) *"From Good to Great: why some companies make the leap and others don't."* Random House

John C. M. (1987) *"Be All You Can Be"* Victor Books.

John C.M (2012) *"The 15 Invaluable Laws of Growth"* New York Boston: Nashville

John C.M (2009) *"How Successful People Think."* Centre Street, Hachette Book .Group

Myles M (2011) "Passing It On." New York Boston: Nashville

Philip S (1876) "Creeds of Christendom, with a History and Critical notes. Volume I. The History of Creeds."

Simon S "How Great Leaders Inspire Action." [online] available at: http://www.ted.com/talks/simon_sinek. (accessed: December 2014)

Smith W (1996) *"The Complete Collections Of His Teachings."* Tulsa, Okla. : Albury Pub.

Steven R. C (1989, 2004) *"The Seven Habits of Highly Effective People"* Great Britain: Simon & Schuster UK Ltd.

KOFI AMOATENG OWUSU

Presents to you, one of the must read books of our time. This book is a ground-breaking manifesto which seeks to answer most of life's questions surrounding everyday living.

Now Available

Amazon.com worldwide in both paperback and kindle.